HOUSE PLANTS
IN COLOUR

Edited by
F B Stark, C B Link and E L Packer

Galley Press

Contents

3 Greenhouse gardening
3 Greenhouses: their purpose
3 Types of greenhouses
4 Siting the greenhouse
4 Heating the greenhouse
4 Temperature control
5 Construction materials
6 The workroom
6 Garden frames
6 Soils
7 Fertilizers
7 Propagation
7   Seed propagation
8   Vegetative propagation
10 Pests
12 Glossary
15 Index of plants mentioned
17 Pteridophytes: selaginellas, ferns
22 Foliage plants
37 Palms
40 Succulents and cacti
53 Flowering plants
60 Orchids

Picture Credits: Peter Way Limited: cover; M. Bavestrelli: 116, 119, 122, 124, 136; C. Bevilacqua: 1, 2, 3, 4, 8, 9, 10, 12, 13, 14, 15, 16, 17, 18, 19, 21, 22, 23, 24, 25, 26, 27, 28, 30, 31, 32, 33, 34, 36, 38, 39, 40, 41, 42, 43, 44, 45, 46, 47, 48, 49, 51, 52, 54, 55, 56, 57, 58, 59, 60, 61, 62, 63, 64, 65, 66, 67, 68, 73, 74, 75, 76, 77, 78, 79, 80, 83, 84, 85, 87, 88, 89, 90, 92, 93, 94, 95, 96, 97, 98, 100, 101, 102, 103, 104, 107, 109, 110, 111, 112, 114, 115, 120, 121, 127, 128, 130, 140, 143, 146, 147, 148, 149, 150, 151, 152, 153, 154, 155, 158, 159, 161, 162, 163, 164, 165, 167, 168, 169, 170, 173, 174, 175, 176, 177, 178, 181, 183, 184, 185, 186; Bravo: 117–126; Etrusko: 139; I.G.D.A.: 5, 6, 11, 20, 29, 50, 53, 69, 72, 106, 108, 123, 129, 131, 133, 141, 156, 157, 160; A. Margiocco: 113, 118; P. Martini: 37, 105, 132; G. Mazza: 7, 145, 166; M. Pedone: 81, 82, 125, 134, 135, 137, 138, 142, 144; P2: 91; P. Popper: 182; S. Prato: 86, 171, 172; F. Quilici: 70; Servizio Giardini Torino: 99, 179, 180.

Adapted from the Italian of Pasquale Perrucchietti
Edited by Francis C. Stark, Conrad B. Link and Edwin Packer

© Orbis Publishing Limited, London 1974
© Istituto Geografico De Agostini, Novara 1969
Published in this edition 1981 by
Galley Press, an imprint of W H Smith and Son Limited
Registered No. 237811 England
Trading as WHS Distributors,
St John's House, East Street,
Leicester, LE1 6NE

Printed in Italy by New Interlitho, Milan
ISBN 0-86136-007-9

Greenhouse gardening

Plants have been associated with man from his very beginnings. He has used them not only for food but for his own personal adornment and for decorating his surroundings. This is well documented in the ruins of ancient buildings, in the uncovered city of Pompeii, and in drawings and paintings down through the centuries. Many works of art and handicrafts of all kinds have designs which are based on plants and flowers; in some cases, the actual reproduction of the plant or flower has been detailed sufficiently to allow for precise identification.

The cultivation of plants and flowers is not only a commercial industry but one which is enjoyed throughout the world by individuals regardless of their social or financial standing. Evidence of man's horticultural involvement is provided by the single geranium plant in the window of a small house, as well by the elaborate garden surrounding a large mansion. Gardening is a very popular hobby and is of interest to people of all ages.

Plants and flowers from the garden not only beautify the surroundings, but many enliven and enhance interior decoration as well. They make our indoor environment more attractive, they add a distinctive touch to any room and help to make the house a home.

Greenhouses offer to the home gardener an opportunity to grow and to work with plants throughout the year.

Greenhouses: their purpose

A greenhouse is a structure covered with a material that transmits light. Traditionally the material has been glass, but in recent years plastics of several kinds and textures have been used. These may be thin films that are useful for only a few months, or rigid materials that are satisfactory for 8 to 10 or more years.

Because the greenhouse is an enclosed structure it is possible to regulate the environment surrounding the plants. It provides us with the opportunity to control light and temperature as well as soil quality, nutrition and water, and hence gives us the ability to establish as specific an environment as may be necessary for the culture of any plant.

The manufacturers of greenhouses have designed many styles and sizes that can be adapted by the greenhouse gardener to meet his requirements in regard to size, shape and usage. The structure may be free standing or attached to the house or garage. The gardener who likes to build may buy one and erect it himself, or he may prefer to design and construct his own.

Types of greenhouses

The conventional greenhouse is rigidly built with a solid foundation and covered with glass or a rigid plastic of a quality to last many years. Such a structure may be constructed of wood and supported with pipe posts or a steel frame, or it may be constructed entirely of aluminium supported with the metal posts. Typically the roof has a uniform slope, although older houses and conservatories may have a slightly curved roof and curved eaves. There are minor variations in the sizes and shapes of the parts of a greenhouse made by different companies.

The size of a greenhouse is adjustable and varies with the manufacturer. Essentially the length is a multiple of the width of the glass that is used on the roof. The side walls should be at least 6 feet tall so as to allow anyone inside to stand erect.

Greenhouse shape is one method of classification. An even-span house is one with an equal slope on either side of the ridge. The section supports may be attached parallel to each other, fastening them at the ridge at the top and at the eave line. This method is referred to as a ridge and furrow construction. The section supports may be separated a uniform distance from each other and attached to a connecting structure or greenhouse; in this arrangement the construction is sometimes referred to as a detached house.

A lean-to greenhouse is essentially one half of an even span house attached in its lengthwise dimension to a building. This shape is common for a domestic greenhouse where it may have the advantage of using the home heating system.

Greenhouse manufacturers are now making both even-span and lean-to style greenhouses designed for a simple foundation that can be erected by the purchaser. Certain of these have large panes of glass extending to the ground level; this allows the light to come in at floor level, giving an opportunity to grow plants under the benches. A greenhouse can have glass right down to the ground or down to low side walls. Some people prefer the former because this type of construction lets in the maximum amount of light in the winter months (the light available in December is only about 10 per cent of that of a June day).

A temporary greenhouse is one usually constructed of lighter structural materials and covered with a plastic film. Such structures are used to extend the growing season either at the beginning, as a method of starting young plants in the spring, or at the end, to protect any plants from early frost in the autumn. For example, temporary greenhouses are used commercially in the spring to start annual plants or in the autumn to prevent a crop of chrysanthemums from being injured by an early frost.

Greenhouses may be classified on the basis of the temperature maintained or the type of plants to be grown. A warm temperature, 20 — 24°C (68–75°F), is used for certain types of orchids, foliage plants, desert plants, or others that need a warm night temperature. A medium temperature house of 16–20°C (60–68°F) or a cool house of 10–12°C (50–53°F) is used for plants requiring lower night temperatures. Certain orchids, cyclamen, poinsettias and dracaenas prefer the medium temperature while carnations would be grown in the cool temperature.

For a domestic greenhouse, where a great variety of plants are to be grown, the style of the structure is not important. Temperature and the light conditions are what matter most and these can be regulated to accommodate the many species of plants in the greenhouse. Fortunately, most plants are tolerant of a wide range of conditions and will grow even if everything in the environment is not to their exact requirements. They may be slower to develop or may not flower as early, but they will grow.

Siting the greenhouse

A north-south direction for the long dimension of the greenhouse is probably the best to obtain maximum light. Modern greenhouses, because of newer styles of construction and the use of larger panes of glass, have less superstructure and thus there is less shadow from the supportive parts; consequently less attention is now paid to the siting. Other factors do enter into the selection of a site, however. Protection provided by other buildings, by walls, a hedge, or a wooded area are all important in reducing wind and air movement. Avoid locations where tall trees or tall structures would shade the greenhouse. If the land slopes, select the slope facing south to take advantage of the greater amount of sun on the greenhouse during the winter months.

These are suggestions that cannot always be acted upon; the beginner will find that he will be able to grow good plants even in a greenhouse that is not ideally sited and may even be more in the shade than the sun. Site cold frames against one side of the greenhouse. For anyone specializing in alpine plants a north-facing cold frame is advisable when establishing cuttings or imported plants.

Heating the greenhouse

Heating systems for the small greenhouse have been designed for efficiency and ease of operation. The system of heating will be influenced by the kind of plants to be grown. Remember that even the warmest temperature needed may be only 20 to 24°C (68–75°F). This requirement is based on the temperature at night and may, in fact, be necessary for only a few kinds of orchids or foliage plants. Other kinds will grow better at a medium temperature of 16 to 18°C (60 to 65°F), and many in still cooler conditions.

It is advisable to rely on the greenhouse manufacturer's recommendations about the heating requirements, which will vary with the temperature requirements for the plants to be grown and with the climate. The number of pipes for a hot water or a steam system, and their location and placement in the house, are influenced by the temperature to be maintained.

A hot water heating system provides steady heat and does not fluctuate suddenly. It is quite easily controlled. A steam system provides heat rapidly and is easily expanded when more greenhouses are built. If the greenhouse is attached to a house, it may be possible to connect either of these systems to the home heating system, and this also applies to a hot air system. Thermostats for greenhouse temperature control should be installed to separate the heat demands of the home from the greenhouse. Often the home will need heat during the daytime while the greenhouse is getting sufficient heat from the sun. During the night when the home temperatures are turned down and outdoor temperatures are lower, the greenhouse will then need the heat.

Greenhouses that are free standing will need their own heating system. This is generally located in the workroom or service building to which they are attached. The heating system can use solid fuel, oil, gas, electricity or paraffin; all have their own advantages and disadvantages. They may be regulated in order to simplify the daily care and attention needed. Electricity is perhaps the simplest system and the provision of paraffin heaters probably the cheapest. Solid fuel systems are also economical in use. There is now available a system whereby the soil itself is heated from below by electricity; this has certain advantages for the gardener, for example he can grow very early crops of lettuce and tomatoes.

Temperature control

A greenhouse is essentially a "heat trap". When the sun hits the glass, the temperature rises rapidly. Even on a cold day, below freezing, if there is little wind the temperatures may be very high and ventilation will be needed. The temperature requirements for a plant are always given in reference to the night temperature. Daytime temperatures are allowed to rise some 10 to 15 degrees higher before ventilation is given. This means that sometimes the night temperature is higher than may be desirable.

WOODEN-FRAME GREENHOUSE

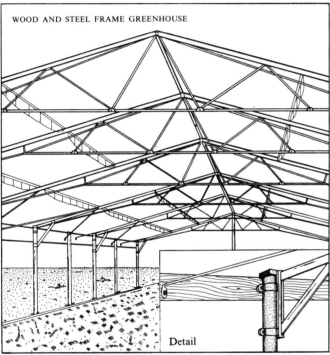

WOOD AND STEEL FRAME GREENHOUSE

Detail

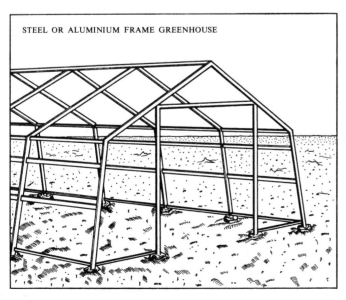

STEEL OR ALUMINIUM FRAME GREENHOUSE

A greenhouse usually has ventilators installed at the ridge and often on the side wall as well. The ridge ventilators may be equipped with an electrically controlled device, activated by a thermostat, to automatically open and close them as the temperature rises or falls.

Exhaust fans may be installed at one end of the house with an opening at the opposite end, thermostatically operated to exhaust the air to the outside when the temperatures are high.

A common practice during the seasons of the year when the temperatures are fairly high and the intensity of light is strong (late spring, summer and early autumn) is to spray or paint the outside of the greenhouse to reduce the light intensity and so reduce the interior temperatures. White-wash, whiting, and diluted water paints are used. Generally they will need to be brushed or scrubbed off in the autumn.

Slat or lath shades, installed in a roller type of arrangement on the outside of the greenhouse, are available. Orchid houses sometimes are shaded with these, and they give an opportunity to regulate the shading from day to day if desirable. Cheesecloth or light grades of muslin suspended in some convenient way may be installed inside over groups of plants.

In areas of low humidity some cooling systems have a pad of a material, such as shavings, that is kept moist; this is installed at one side of the house with an exhaust fan on the opposite side to allow the air to be drawn through the house. In this process of moving the moist air, the air inside the greenhouse is cooled to some degree. This is less effective in regions of a naturally high humidity than in areas where the summer air is normally fairly dry.

Construction materials

The most modern greenhouses are now using extruded aluminium for all supportive parts of the structure. In larger houses, some of the superstructure may be of steel. Aluminium is slightly more expensive than wood but is cheaper in the long run. It is durable and does not need painting.

When steel is used for supports it should be galvanized to reduce maintenance and add to its durability.

Wood for greenhouses is generally cedar wood, oak or softwood. When additionally protected with paint all are satisfactory. Repainting will be necessary from time to time. Though more expensive, cedar wood is preferable to soft-wood. When painting wood, use a good quality white oil-base paint that does not contain any mercury fungicidal material. Aluminium paints are sometimes used, but they do not reflect the light as well as white paint. The heating pipes in a greenhouse are not usually painted.

Glass panes are the customary material for glazing, although polyethylene and polyvinyl are used. These are effective for 8 to 12 months, but are easily damaged by storms and heavy winds. Rigid types of plastic materials are available in panels, often large enough to extend from the ridge to the eave without a joint, making a leakproof roof.

A greenhouse should be provided with water and electricity. Water is generally available from the same source as that which supplies the house. Faucets should be located in one or more places to attach a hose for watering. Automatic water systems are possible for a domestic greenhouse and, once they have been installed, reduce the daily chores. Water should also be available to use in a mist system.

While an electrical source is not essential for a greenhouse, it becomes necessary if automatic controls for heating or a mist system are used, and for circulating fans. Supplementary lighting is necessary if certain plants are to be grown out of season and in those cases where long days are necessary for flower formation and development. Much progress has been made in recent years with artificial-light gardening.

The workroom

A service area is necessary to operate a small greenhouse and this is generally in a workroom attached to it, or if the greenhouse is attached to the house or garage then work space should be provided close at hand. The workroom would include space for the heating system if there is need for a separate system.

The workroom should include a work table and cupboards or shelves for storing supplies, for tools and equipment, and for such items as pots, pesticides, extra soil and organic materials. Pesticides should be stored in a place that can be locked.

The exterior of the workroom should, of course, be of a style or design to fit in with other buildings.

Garden frames

In addition to the conventional greenhouse, glass- or plastic-covered frames may provide additional growing space for propagation, for starting young plants, or for storage or certain plants over the winter. If heat is supplied to such frames, they are sometimes referred to as hot beds; without heating they are called cold frames.

Garden frames are obtainable either in one or two-light designs, of varying dimensions but not usually exceeding 8 feet in length, 6 feet in width, 10 inches in height at the front and 20 inches at the back. Shallow frames, known as Dutch Light Frames, used for the propagation of bedding plants and lettuces, are constructed with from one to five lights according to need.

Soils

In selecting a soil for the growing of plants in the greenhouse, choose one with a good texture, loose and crumb-like. Soils that have had turf growing on them for at least a year or more generally have a good structure. If the soil is a loam, so much the better. Clay soils are usable if they have a good structure although they are likely to loose it rather quickly. Sandy soils have a loose texture. Fertility can be added to

the soil later but the soil structure cannot be changed.

Modern greenhouse practices are developing more towards the use of soil mixtures, such as John Innes composts. Generally these are a combination of a soil plus organic matter and perhaps including some inert material.

Many gardeners today make use of these prepared composts that take a great deal of hard work out of greenhouse culture. Not only are the constituents accurately measured, they are also sterile and so free from fungoid diseases, weed seeds and pests. But this ideal condition will be lost if the compost is allowed to stand in the greenhouse or out of doors, exposed to the air. Once the bag has been opened it should be stored in a covered container.

A composted soil can be made in the garden by building a pile of alternate layers of soil and organic materials. This organic matter may be leaves, garden refuse, straw, animal manures or any inexpensive organic material. After such a pile has been established for 6 to 8 months it is ready for use. Break it up in such a manner that the soil and organic matter are mixed. To speed up the process of rotting, the pile may even be broken up and rebuilt before using. Fertilizers such as superphosphate and even some nitrogen forms may be included as the pile is built. A compost heap would be a way in which the gardener could re-use soil from old plants.

Soil mixtures are made as needed. These are mixtures of a soil, an organic matter such as peat, and, if a very loose final product is needed, sand, perlite or vermiculite. The proportion of each can be varied, but a mixture of equal parts by volume of each gives good results.

Organic matter for greenhouse soils is usually peat. Decomposed leaves may be available, and depending on location other things can be obtained such as decomposed animals manures, straw and various grasses. Peat is convenient for the home gardener because it is essentially sterile, free of weed seed and easy to handle.

Soils or soil mixtures for most plants should be slightly acid. The pH formula is used to express the acidity or alkalinity of the soil; pH7 is the neutral point, below it being acid and above it alkaline. If the soil or the soil mixture has a soil reaction with a pH of 6.0 or lower, then lime should be added during preparation. Only a few plants, such as azaleas, rhododendrons, gardenia, and *Erica* will want an acid soil.

Certain orchids, especially the epiphytic kinds, are not grown in soil but in osmunda fibre, which is the fibrous roots and stem of the Osmunda fern, or in bracken or turf fibre. The terrestrial types are grown in soil mixtures usually having a very high percentage of organic matter and often using sphagnum moss and a shredded bark.

Several commercially-prepared soil mixtures are being sold for greenhouse use. They are primarily a mixture of peat and perlite or vermiculite, thoroughly mixed and of a uniform grade. These are packaged in conveniently sized bags and may be used for seed and vegetative propagation, as well as for general potting. Much research has gone into perfecting these excellent mixtures.

Fertilizers

Nitrogen, phosphorus and potassium are the three nutrient elements that are essential to plant growth and flowering. Such materials may be added in a dry form as the soil is prepared or in a liquid form after the plant has been planted. The liquid types are water soluble and may be applied in very dilute concentrations every time the plant is watered or in a more concentrated form less frequently. The inorganic fertilizers, in either the dry or liquid form, may supply only one element or, in certain cases, two elements. Commercial mixtures generally supply the three nutrient elements named and often include one or more of the trace elements such as iron, boron, or manganese which, in very minute quantities, are necessary for plant growth.

The inorganic fertilizers are the least expensive to use when based on the amount of nutrients they supply. Organic fertilizers are not available to the plant until they have been decomposed.

Inorganic fertilizer sources are those manufactured especially or are by-products of certain manufacturing processes. They include ammonium sulphate, calcium sulphate, sodium nitrate, ammonium nitrate, and urea that supply nitrogen; superphosphate that supplies phosphorus; and potassium chloride or potassium sulphate that supply potassium.

The organic fertilizers are produced primarily as a by-product from certain animals. Organic nitrogen sources include horn and hoof shavings, dried blood and fish meal; phosphorus may be supplied from bonemeal; and wood ashes are an organic source of potassium. Organic fertilizers may vary slightly from time to time in the exact amount of fertilizer element they supply, and may actually contribute traces of some other elements when decomposing. This is due to the process employed when making the fertilizer.

Lime is not considered to be a fertilizer; its value is that it makes the soil less acid and helps improve soil structure. Calcium does become available to the plant from the lime incorporated in the soil.

Animals manures are not easily available, and are variable as to their fertility value which is influenced by the kind of animal, its diet, the amount of bedding material included, and the care of the manure before application to the soil. The greatest value of manure is not as a fertilizer, but rather as a source of organic matter which has a beneficial influence on improving soil structure.

In a well-constructed greenhouse with a tight roof, there is little air change if the ventilators are closed. Under winter conditions, with a heavy mass of plant growth in the house, a bright sun, and actively growing plants, it is possible that the carbon dioxide content of the air in the greenhouse may become insufficient for good plant growth. It has been found that growth is increased by injecting carbon dioxide into the atmosphere. This is done commercially under selected conditions. For a domestic greenhouse, this practice is probably not necessary.

For the average gardener it will be most convenient to use commercially-prepared fertilizers, which are usually mixtures of materials that supply nitrogen, phosphorus, and potassium and are referred to as "complete fertilizers". They are available both in a dry form to be mixed into the soil in advance of planting or as a top dressing, or are made of water-soluble materials that can be dissolved in water and applied to the soil in liquid form.

Another fertilizer is the slow-release or slow-acting kind that may be mixed into the soil and remains effective for many months. One form is a soluble material encapsulated in a plastic-like material which, when in contact with the soil moisture, gradually releases the fertilizer that then becomes available to the plant.

Propagation

Propagation of plants is possible by two methods:
1. By the seed—the sexual method.
2. By vegetative means—the asexual methods. There are many forms of this; the form to use varies with different plants. For some plants only one method is effective while for other plants several methods may be used.

Seed propagation

Seed is the method generally used for propagation of the species and for any plant that will come "true-to-type" by this method; that is, where the seedling will produce a plant similar to the plant from which it came. Seed is used in breeding programmes where plants of different genetic make-ups are crossed in order to obtain new kinds.

Some seeds are sown in the area where they are to grow. Plants that do not transplant easily are handled in this way. Among ornamental plants, this method is necessary for only a few kinds of annuals. Most seed is sown in a medium that is loose, porous, well aerated and yet will hold water. Such a medium can be prepared by mixing soil with organic matter and perhaps some inert material. In outdoor beds this may be accomplished by merely selecting a suitable spot with well-drained soil. Mixtures of materials include peat and perlite, peat and vermiculite, or other mixtures that include soil, sand or similar inert substances; they can be bought from seedsmen in prepared mixtures if necessary.

Seed may be sown in beds out of doors or in the home at a window, in a greenhouse, or in protective frames such as a cold frame or hot bed. It should be scattered over the seed bed uniformly and then lightly covered. Tiny seeds such as those of begonia, calceolaria, petunia, or azalea are not covered, but are merely pressed into the soil. For seeds of this kind, covering the soil with a thin layer of finely-screened sphagnum makes a good material for the seed.

When the seed has germinated, thin out the weak seedlings and those that are crowded to allow those remaining to have greater space for development. When the seedlings have developed their first true leaf they are ready for transplanting. Transplant them to seed beds, spacing them to allow for development, and then later transplant them again to where they are to grow. Or they may be transplanted to pots or other containers. Rapidly-growing kinds are often transplanted from the seed bed to the place where they are to grow to maturity.

In recent years the use of pelleted seed has grown both in commercial horticulture and domestic gardening. Pellets make seeds much easier to handle and sow, consequently less thinning is necessary. A prerequisite for success with pelleted seed is moist soil, for moisture causes the pellet to distintegrate so that germination can commence. Watering is therefore essential before and after sowing.

separation into smaller parts, by layering, or by grafting or budding.

Tubers, bulbs, rhizomes and runners are essentially modified stems which can produce new roots when separated from the mother plant. Once removed, they can be immediately replanted.

Layering is a form of propagation where a branch is bent down to the soil and covered, leaving the tip exposed. Often a wound is made in the stem portion that is covered. After roots develop, the branch is cut at the end nearest the parent and the new plant is replanted. Air layering is a method often used on foliage plants that have become too tall. A wound is

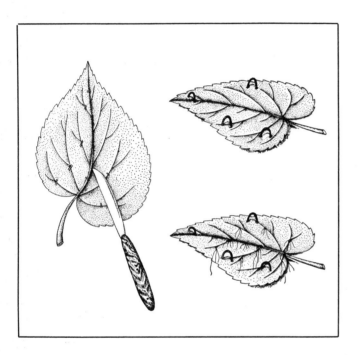

Preparation of a leaf cutting. On the left, make small incisions through the veins on the underside of the leaf. On the right above, the leaf is stretched out and made fast to the soil with hairpins. On the right below, the adventitious roots are seen developing.

Propagation by division of a plant.

Vegetative propagation

Since plants produced from seed may not come true-to-type or may require too long a period of time before coming into flower or developing mature characteristics, a vegetative method is often used. Plants vary in the part of the plant that may be used for propagation; depending on the kind of plant, it may be the stem, leaves, or the roots. In some plants, vegetative methods merely use the parts of the plant that naturally account for the increase, such as the bulbs, tubers, rhizomes, stolons, or off-shoot runners. This is, of course, extremely convenient for the gardener. Propagation may also be achieved by dividing of the plant which involves its

made in the stem, a bit of wood is placed in the wound to hold it open, and the wound is dusted with a root-promoting hormone. The entire area is covered with moist sphagnum moss and wrapped with plastic or aluminium foil. The moss must be kept moist. After roots have developed into the moss, the stem is severed below this area and the tip with developing roots is potted as a new plant. The technique of air layering can also be used to propagate some woody plants outdoors.

Cuttings are perhaps the most common method of vegetative propagation. Cuttings are made from strong, healthy stems. The tip is used generally with 3 to 4 nodes, varying with the kind of plant; often similar sections of the lower portions of the stem can be selected as well. The season of propagation varies with the plant. Soft immature growth is not satisfactory, that selected should be fully developed, although it does not need to be fully mature. Such growth is referred to as a soft-wood cutting or as a greenwood or herbaceous cutting. Other cuttings may be semi-woody or fully developed and woody. Cuttings are propagated in sand, peat, perlite, vermiculite or some other inert, pest-free material. Some gardeners make a mixture of these. Loose porous soil is also used, especially when propagating, outdoors.

Commercial preparations of these are available in either a dry or liquid form. The dry form is a hormone powder, and the stem end is dipped into it before it is placed in the propagative medium. The liquid kinds are either ready to use or need to be diluted with water. In either case, the stem end is dipped into or soaked in the solution before being put in the medium. These preparations are available in small sized packages for the home gardener. They contain chemicals such as indole-acetic acid, indole-butyric acid, or salts of these acids with other related chemicals.

The leaves from certain types of plants may be used for propagation. Mature leaves are removed from a plant such

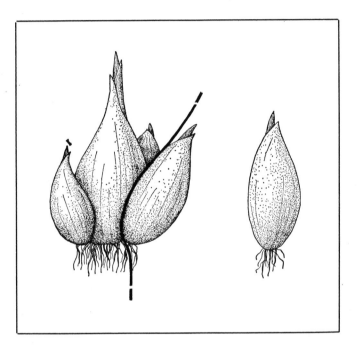

Division of small bulbs surrounding a mature bulb.

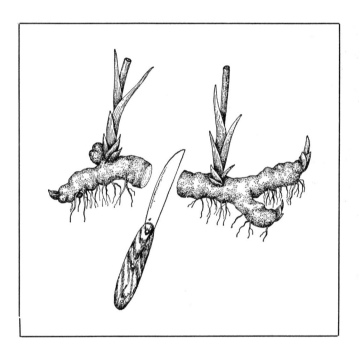

Propagation by division of a rhizome.

In the greenhouse, propagation is done in a shaded location, either by shading the plants or the glass above them. The humidity should be high. The use of a misting system to keep the cuttings moist is recommended. It can be made automatic, thus reducing the attention needed. During the autumn, winter and spring months the rooting of many cuttings is hastened if the medium is several degrees warmer than the air temperature. Heating pipes located below the propagation bench or the use of an electric heating cable are ways in which this can be accomplished and controlled.

Root-promoting chemicals speed up the time of rooting and ensure that a higher percentage of cuttings will root.

as *Saintpaulia* and inserted into a propagating medium in the same manner as a stem cutting. A new plant will develop at the base and when it is large enough to handle conveniently, it is potted as a new plant. Leaves of peperomias may be handled in the same way. Leaves of certain begonias, especially *Begonia Rex*, are laid on a moist propagative medium and new plants will develop at the base as well as at any wound that is made in the large leaf veins (see the illustration on the left-hand side of p. 8). Leaves of the *Sansevieria* may be cut into sections 2 to 3 inches long and treated in the same way.

Division is a simple method of propagation. It is used for

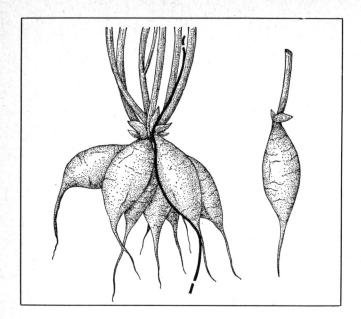

Propagation by division of a tuberous root.

those plants that form a cluster of many stems, and is demonstrated in the illustrations on pages 9 and 10. The plant is removed from the pot and the stems or crowns are cut apart into smaller pieces. Usually this is done when the plant is in its least active period of growth. The practice is the same as that used for perennial plants outdoors.

Grafting and the related technique of budding are seldom used for greenhouse plants. An appropriate understock is selected, and a scion of the desired plant is attached or the bud inserted. The methods of caring for the grafted or budded plants, and the season of the year for propagation, vary with the kind of plant. Fruit trees, some azaleas, roses and lilacs are familiar plants that are grafted. Cacti are sometimes grafted, to produce odd-shaped plants; an example is the practice of grafting the Christmas Cactus, *Schlumbergera* or *Zygocactus*, onto *Pereskia* to form a tree-like plant.

Pests

Plants in the greenhouse are subjected to pests just as they are out of doors. In some respects it is easier to control the pests in a greenhouse since there is a rapid plant growth. The foliage may be kept dry, which can be important in preventing disease, and having the plants enclosed gives an opportunity to fumigate or use an aerosol pesticide.

There are several major groups of pests and diseases that attack plants in the greenhouse.

Plants which suffer from physiological problems often appear as if they have been affected by an insect or a disease. Leaf damage or irregularities may be caused by a mineral deficiency or excess, especially of the three major elements most commonly needed by plants (nitrogen, phosphorus and potassium) and on occasion of other elements such as magnesium or boron. A lack of each element produces a distinctive reaction in the plant, yet the deficiency is some-sometimes difficult to diagnose since some diseases may also show similar symptoms. Toxic substances in the atmosphere may cause marginal injury to leaves or interfere with normal leaf development.

Improper conditions in the environment, such as excess or insufficient light for a given plant, may cause unnatural growth, resulting in foliage that is excessively large or small or an unnatural leaf colour for that plant. Constant excess or insufficient water in the soil will influence plant growth, and eventually the size and perhaps flower formation as well. Soil deficiencies are corrected by the proper fertilizer applications; excess applications can be leached from the soil by frequent, heavy watering provided the soil has good drainage.

Oedema, the development of swellings or outgrowths on the lower side of the leaf of certain plants, is associated with an excessive supply of water in the soil and high humidity in the greenhouse. It is peculiarly a greenhouse problem.

The more typical diseases include the virus diseases and those caused by bacteria or by fungi.

Virus diseases are caused by a submicroscopic organism that increases rapidly in the sap of the infected plant. They are spread by contact with an affected plant. Because the vascular system is infected there is generally no control possible. Some virus diseases develop so rapidly that the plant is dwarfed and shows characteristic leaf patterns of green and yellow. A few virus diseases seem not to do much damage and may be present without injury. This is true for some variegated plants, where the variegation is actually caused by a virus. Most virus diseases are specific for a given plant while others may infect many kinds. There are no effective controls for viruses, hence use care in selecting propagation material and get rid of infected plants.

Bacterial diseases develop when bacteria enter the plant through a wound and cause damage. Most rot or decaying diseases are caused by bacteria, as well as certain leaf spots, leaf blights and galls.

Fungi cause other types of injury, again they may appear as a leaf spot, or leaf blight, as cankers on a stem, as mildew or as rust on a leaf stem. Diseases that cause the plant to wilt are also caused by fungi.

Damping off, the dying of seedlings and young plants by rotting at the soil line or just below, may be caused by several disease organisms. Soil sterilization and seed or soil treatment with fungicide are effective controls, together with the avoidance of stuffy, damp conditions.

For the control of disease in a greenhouse, first be certain that the soil and environment are correct for the plant, then remove infected parts if possible and use a recommended fungicide, following the directions. Disease controls are constantly changing, but currently recommended fungicides are to be found in the catalogues of seedsmen.

Insect pests include many of the same kinds found outdoors, such as aphids, thrips, scale and leaf chewing insects, white fly, and spider mites. Insects may attack many kinds of plants, in contrast to certain diseases that attack only one species or closely-related species.

Aphids typically are found on rapidly-growing tips of plants and injure the plant by sucking the juices. Thrips are very tiny and feed on the underside of the leaf, sucking the juices and causing a silvery appearance on the surface. Scale insects are sucking insects that attach themselves to stems and leaves and are covered with a waxy or shell-like covering which makes them more difficult to control. Mealy bugs are soft white insects, "mealy" in appearance, found in the axils of the leaves and at the tip, and cause damage by sucking the plant sap. Control is difficult because of this waxy covering. Cyclamen mites attack the growing shoots of the African violet, cyclamen, begonia, gloxinia and other gesneriads, causing the new growth to be stunted or deformed, and preventing the plant from developing properly. White fly is a small white insect from the tropics and can become difficult to control. The adults are moth-like, covered with a white waxy powder and fly about when the plant is disturbed. This insect lays its eggs on the underside of the leaves of many greenhouse plants; the immature stages are a pale greenish colour, semi-transparent and cause damage by sucking the plant juices. Lantana, cineraria, fuchsia, ageratum, tomatoes, and poinsettias are favourites of this insect.

The control of insects involves using a spray or dust. The recommended materials change so rapidly to conform to acceptable safety standards that commercial preparations have become the most convenient method of control. Many insects are most easily destroyed when immature; plants should be thoroughly covered with the insecticide both on the top and the lower side of the leaf. It is a good greenhouse practice to inspect all plants before they are brought into the greenhouse and to spray them. Sometimes a thorough washing of the foliage with warm soapy water will dislodge the pests; this is then followed by clear water to remove the suds. Syringing of the plants with water will dislodge many insects, and if it is done routinely may give control, especially during seasons when insects cannot come in from outdoors.

There is still another group of pests, not true insects but for practical purposes often considered with them, that will cause damage. These include woodlice, oval-shaped pests with many legs, that curl into a ball when disturbed. Millipedes also have many legs, are typically shiny dark brown and move rapidly. These pests are found under seed trays, pots, and in dark areas where they feed on decaying organic matter; they are usually harmless to growing plants. However, when numerous they may attack seedlings and young plants. Slugs or slimy snails without a shell, and snails with a shell, may be a greenhouse nuisance because they feed not only on decaying matter but on seedlings or on soft succulent leaves and new growth. Control for these is by using baits, such as metaldehyde or slug pellets.

Eel worms are another soil pest that may attack the roots or the leaves. These are also called nematodes; they penetrate the tissue and in the case of roots may cause a swelling or an enlargement. Foliage eel worms create damage by causing spots or sections of a leaf to turn brown, as on begonias or chrysanthemums. For soil eel worms, soil sterilization is the best control; the planting of pest-free material is of course advantageous. Foliar types are controlled by sprays.

Glossary

*see illustration

*1. **Achene**—a dry, hard, indehiscent, single-seeded fruit with a single carpel.

2. **Acaulescent**—stemless

3. **Acuminate**—tapering to a point.

4. **Adnate**—united, grown together.

5. **Adventitious**—originating at other than the usual place; *roots* originating from any structure other than a root; *buds* arising from a part of the plant other than terminal or node.

6. **Alternate** (leaves)—one leaf at each node but alternating in direction.

7. **Annual**—a plant with a one-year life cycle.

8. **Anther**—that part of the stamen containing the pollen.

9. **Apetalous**—lacking petals.

10. **Apical**—terminal or summit.

11. **Axil**—the angle between a leaf and stem.

*12. **Berry**—a simple, fleshy fruit developed from a single ovule (loosely, any pulpy or juicy fruit).

13. **Biennial**—a plant with a two-year life cycle.

14. **Blade**—the expanded part of a leaf or leaflet.

*15. **Blossom**—the flower of a seed plant.

16. **Bract**—a specialized, modified leaf; of leaf-like structure.

17. **Bud**—a compressed stem; an underdeveloped stem.

18. **Bulb**—underground storage and reproductive organ with fleshy leaves called bulb scales.

19. **Calyx**—the outermost of the floral parts, composed of sepals.

*20. **Campanulate**—bell-shaped.

21. **Capitate**—shaped like a head.

*22. **Capsule**—a dry, dehiscent, multi-seeded fruit of more than one carpel.

23. **Carpel**—a leaf-like structure bearing ovules along the margins; a simple pistil.

*24. **Cauline**—related to an obvious stem or axis.

25. **Comose**—having tufts of hair.

*26. **Cordate**—heart-shaped.

27. **Corm**—an enlarged, underground stem, serving as a storage organ for food reserves.

28. **Corolla**—an inner cycle of floral organs, comprising the petals.

29. **Corymb**—a flat-topped, indeterminate flower cluster, with pedicels originating along a central peduncle; outer flowers open first.

30. **Cotyledons**—the first (seed) leaves of the embryo.

31. **Crenate**—toothed with rounded teeth.

32. **Crispate**—curled.

33. **Culm**—the stem of a grass or sedge.

34. **Cultivar**—a variety developed from known hybridization or origin.

35. **Cuneate**—triangular, wedge-shaped.

36. **Cyme**—a determinate flower cluster in which the central flower opens first.

37. **Deciduous**—plants that drop their leaves at the end of each season.

38. **Dehiscent**—opening of an anther or a fruit, permitting escape of pollen or seeds.

39. **Dentate**—toothed along the margins, apex sharp.

40. **Dichotomous**—divided into pairs; forked branches roughly equal.

41. **Dicotyledonous**—having two cotyledons.

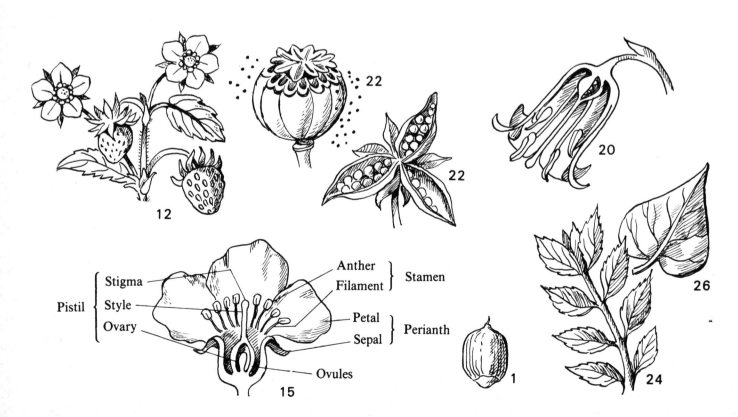

42. **Digitate** (leaves)—with leaflets arising from the apex of the petiole.

43. **Dioecious**—a species having male and female flowers on different, individual plants.

44. **Distichous**—in two vertical ranks, as the leaves of grasses.

*45. **Drupe**—a simple fleshy fruit, single carpel, with a hard endocarp containing the seed, e.g., the peach.

46. **Embryo**—a rudimentary plant.

47. **Entire**—without dentation or division.

48. **Epiphyte**—a plant that grows on another but is not parasitic.

49. **Fasciated**—an abnormally wide and flat stem.

50. **Filament**—the part of the stamen supporting the anther.

51. **Follicle**—a dry, dehiscent fruit with a single carpel, which dehisces along the ventral suture.

52. **Frond**—the leaf of a fern.

53. **Glabrous**—without hairs or pubescence.

54. **Glaucous**—covered with a whitish "bloom."

55. **Habit**—the general appearance of a plant.

*56. **Head**—a short, dense inflorescence, frequently with ray flowers around the margins and *tubular* disk flowers inside.

57. **Herbaceous**—non-woody.

58. **Hirsute**—hairy.

59. **Humus**—incompletely decomposed organic materials in the soil.

60. **Hybrid**—the result of a cross between two parents differing in genetic composition.

61. **Hydrophyte**—water loving; a plant adapted to wet conditions; capable of growing in water.

62. **Imbricate**—overlapping vertically or spirally.

63. **Indehiscent**—fruits remaining closed at maturity.

64. **Inflorescence**—the arrangement of flowers in a cluster; a complete flower cluster.

65. **Internode**—the part of a stem between two nodes.

66. **Involucre**—a cycle of bracts subtending a flower or an inflorescence.

67. **Keel**—the two front, united petals of most leguminous flowers, e.g., pea.

*68. **Lanceolate**—lance-shaped, narrow and tapered at the ends, widening above the base and narrowed to the apex.

*69. **Legume**—dry, dehiscent fruit, single carpel, usually opening along both sutures.

70. **Lenticils**—small, corky areas on woody stems.

71. **Lenticular**—lens-shaped.

72. **Ligulate**—strap-shaped.

73. **Ligule**—a thin membrane at the top of the leaf sheath in the grasses.

74. **Lip**—one portion of an unequally divided corolla; often of different sizes or colors as in orchids.

75. **Monoecious**—having male and female flowers on the same plant.

76. **Morphology**—form, structure, and development.

77. **Needle**—the long, narrow leaf characteristic of the conifers, as pine and spruce.

78. **Node**—point on a stem from which a leaf or branch emerges.

*79. **Opposite** (leaves)—two leaves at each node, opposite each other.

*80. **Palmate**—palm-like, radiating outward from the base.

*81. **Panicle**—a compound raceme.

*82. **Papilionaceous** (corolla)—a pea-like flower, having a standard keel and wings.

83. **Pedicel**—the stem of a single flower.

84. **Peduncle**—the stem of an inflorescence.

85. **Perennial**—a plant that lives from year to year and does not die after fruiting.

86. **Perfect** (flower)—having both stamens and carpels in the same flower.

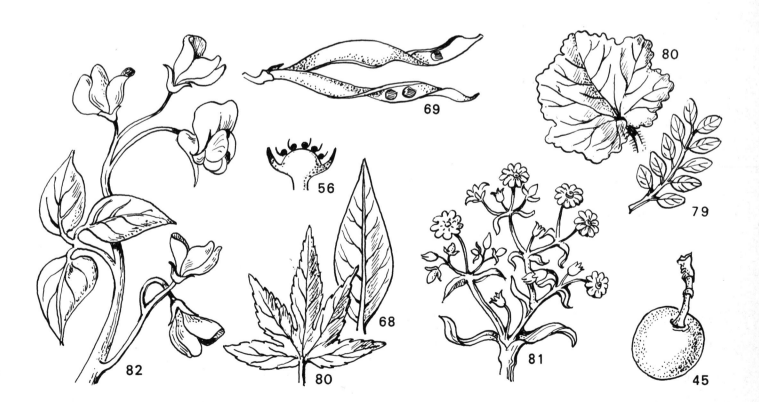

87. **Perianth**—the calyx and corolla.
88. **Persistent**—remaining attached.
89. **Petal**—one member of the corolla.
90. **Petiole**—the supporting stalk of the leaf blade.
91. **Pinnate**—separate leaflets arranged along a leaf stalk.
92. **Pistil**—the female reproductive parts of a flower, comprised of the stigma, style, and ovary.
*93. **Pome**—a fleshy, indehiscent fruit, with a leathery endocarp surrounding the seed, e.g., the apple.
94. **Pseudobulb**—thickened bulblike structure on leaves of epiphytic orchids.
95. **Pubescent**—covered with short hairs; downy.
96. **Raceme**—an elongated, indeterminate flower cluster with each floret on a pedicel.
97. **Rachis**—the axis of a spike.
98. **Receptacle**—the axis of a flower stalk bearing the floral parts.
99. **Reniform**—kidney-shaped.
100. **Reticulate**—as in a network of veins in a leaf.
101. **Rhizome**—an underground stem, usually horizontal, from which shoots and roots may develop.
102. **Rosette**—a cluster of leaves crowded on very short internodes.
103. **Rugose**—wrinkled.
104. **Sagittate**—arrow-shaped.
*105. **Samara**—a dry, indehiscent fruit having a wing, e.g., maple.
*106. **Scape**—a leafless flower stem arising from the soil.
107. **Schizocarp**—a dry, dehiscent fruit in which the carpels separate at maturation.
108. **Sepal**—a single member of the calyx.
109. **Septum**—a partition within an organ.
*110. **Serrate**—with sharp teeth and directed forward.

111. **Sessile**—without a stalk.
112. **Silique**—a dry, dehiscent fruit with two carpels separated by a septum.
113. **Sori**—spore masses on a fern.
*114. **Spadix**—a spike with a thick, fleshy axis, usually enveloped by a spathe.
*115. **Spathe**—a large bract or bracts surrounding an inflorescence.
116. **Spatulate**—spade-shaped; oblong with the basal end narrow.
*117. **Spike**—an inflorescence like a raceme except the florets are sessile to the peduncle.
118. **Stamen**—the male organ that bears the pollen.
119. **Standard** (in a papilionaceous corolla)—the large upper petal.
120. **Stigma**—the receptive part of the female organ.
121. **Stipule**—an appendage at the base of the petiole in some species.
122. **Stolon**—a prostrate stem that tends to root; sometimes called a runner.
123. **Style**—that part of the pistil connecting the stigma and the ovary.
124. **Succulent**—fleshy and juicy.
125. **Terrestrial**—plants growing in soil.
126. **Tomentose**—densely covered with hairs; woolly.
127. **Tuber**—underground storage organ; a stem with buds, e.g., the potato.
*128. **Umbel**—an indeterminate inflorescence in which the pedicels originate at about the same point on the peduncle and are about the same length, e.g., flowers of carrot.
*129. **Undulate**—a wavy surface.
130. **Variety**—a subdivision of a species, naturally occurring.
131. **Whorled**—leaves arranged in a circle around the stem.
132. **Wings**—(in a papilionaceous corolla)—the two side petals.
133. **Xerophyte**—a plant adapted to dry, arid conditions.

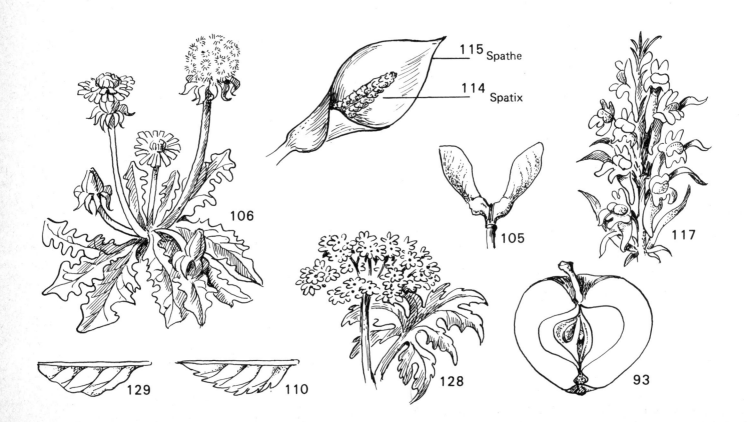

Index of plants mentioned

Acanthocereus 48
Acineta 61
Adiantum birkenheadii 18
Adiantum Capillus-Veneris 18
Adiantum cuneatum 18
Adiantum pedatum 18
Adiantum peruvianum 18
Adiantum rhodophyllum 18
Adiantum rubellum 18
Adiantum tenerum 18
Adiantum trapeziforme 18
Aechmea fasciata 32
Aechmea fulgens 32
African violet 56
Aichryson 41
Aloë 44, 45
Aloë africana 44
Aloë arborescens 45
Aloë brevifolia 45
Aloë ciliaris 44
Aloë ferox 45
Aloë humilis 45
Aloë perfoliata 44
Aloë striata 45
Aloë variegata 45
Aloë vera 45
Alternanthera 64
Anthurium Andreanum 53
Anthurium crystallinum 53
Anthurium Kalbreyeri 53
Anthurium misquelianum 53
Anthurium Scherzerianum 53
Anthurium Veitchii 53
Aphelandra aurantiaca 31
Aphelandra fascinator 31
Aphelandra squarrosa 31
Aphelandra tetragona 31
Aralia 23
Arecastrum Romanzoffianum 38
Asparagus asparagoides 24
Asparagus plumosus 24
Asparagus Sprengeri 24
Asparagus verticillatus 24
Aspidistra elatior 22
Asplenium Belangeri 20
Asplenium bulbiferum 20
Asplenium caudatum 20
Asplenium Nidus-Avis 20
Asplenium radicans 20
Asplenium Ruta-muraria 20
Asplenium sandersoni 20
Asplenium seelosii 20
Asplenium trichomanes 20
Asplenium viviparum 20
Azalea 59
Begonia 26, 63
Begonia asplenifolia 26
Begonia metallica 26
Begonia Rex 26
Begonia Scharffii 26
Begonia semperflorens 26, 63
Begonia socotrana 26
Begonia tuberybrida 26
Begonia veitchii 26
Bilbergia 32
Bressavola 61
Bryophyllum 41
Caladium bicolor 33
Caladium Humboldtii 33

Caladium picturatum 33
Caladium Schomburgkii 33
Calathea insignis 36
Calathea Mackoyana 36
Calathea ornata 36
Calathea roseo-picta 36
Calathea Veitchiana 36
Calathea zebrina 36
Calla 54
Carpobrotus acinaciformis 46
Carpobrotus edulis 46
Cattleya 61
Cephalocereus lanuginosus 49
Cephalocereus Royenii 49
Cephalocereus Russelianus 49
Cephalocereus senilis 49
Cereus azureus 48
Cereus peruvianus 48
Cereus varabelis 48
Chamaedorea elatior 39
Chamaedorea Ernesti-Augusti 39
Chamaedorea Pacaya 39
Chamaedorea Tapejilote 39
Chamaerops humilis 37, 38
Cocos 38
Codiaeum variegatum 34
Coelogyne 61
Coleus 64
Collinia elegans 37, 39
Cordyline indivisa 29
Cordyline terminalis 29
Cotyledon 41
Crassula arborescens 41
Crassula argentea 41
Crassula falcata 41
Crassula lactea 41
Crassula perfoliata 41
Crassula sarcocaulis 41
Croton 34
Cryophytum crystallinum 46
Cryptanthus 32
Cycas revoluta 39
Cymbidium 61, 62, 63
Cymbidium grandiflorum 62
Cymbidium insigne 62
Cymbidium Lowianum 62
Cypripedium 60, 62, 63
Cypripedium barbatum 63
Cypripedium delenatii 63
Cypripedium faireanum 63
Cypripedium insigne 63
Date palm 39
Dieffenbachia picta 35
Dieffenbachia Seguine 35
Dizygotheca elegantissima 23
Dorotheanthus bellidiformis 46
Dracaena arborea 29
Dracaena deremensis 29
Dracaena Draco 29
Dracaena fragrans 29
Dracaena Godseffiana 29
Dracaena Goldieana 29
Dracaena Hookeriana 29
Echeveria 41, 43
Echeveria agavoides 43
Echeveria elegans 43
Echeveria glauca 43
Echeveria multicaulis 43
Echeveria setosa 43

Echinocactus 48, 51
Echinocatus Grusonii 51
Echinocactus horizonthalonius 51
Echinocactus ingens 51
Echinopsis 48
Epiphyllum Ackermanii 52
Epiphyllum oxypetalum 52
Euphorbia abyssinica 55
Euphorbia fulgens 55
Euphorbia pulcherrima 55
Euphorbia resinifera 55
Euphorbia splendens 55
Euphorbia tridentata 55
Fatshedera Lizei 23
Fatsia japonica 23
Ferns 18, 19, 20, 21, 24
Ficus carica 28
Ficus diversifolia 28
Ficus elastica 28
Ficus lyrata 29
Ficus pumila 28
Ficus repens 28
Ficus Sycomorus 28
Geranium 58, 63
Gusmania 32
Haworthia fasciata 45
Haworthia margaritifera 45
Haworthia retusa 45
Haworthia rigida 45
Haworthia tessellata 45
Haworthia tortuosa 45
Hottentot Fig 46
Houlletia 61
Howea Belmoreana 37
Howea Forsteriana 37
Hoya bandaensis 57
Hoya bella 57
Hoya carnosa 57
Hoya globulosa 57
Hoya imperialis 57
Hoya multiflora 57
Kalanchoë 41, 42
Kalanchoë beharensis 42
Kalanchoë lanceolata 42
Kalanchoë Blossfeldiana 42
Kalanchoë lacinata 42
Kalanchoë flammea 42
Kalanchoë marmorata 42
Kalanchoë pinnata 42
Kalanchoë thyrsiflora 42
Kentia 37
Lady slipper 62
Laelia albida 61
Laelia anceps 61
Laelia crispa 61
Laelia pumila 61
Laelia purpurata 61
Laelio Cattleya 61
Lampranthus roseus 46
Maidenhair Fern 18
Mamillaria arida 50
Mamillaria carnea 50
Mamillaria fragilis 50
Mamillaria longicorna 50
Mamillaria microcarpa 50
Mamillaria prolifera 50
Mamillaria pusilla 50
Mamillaria spinosissima 50
Mamillaria triangularis 50

Mamillaria uncinata 50
Maranta arundinacea 36
Maranta bicolor 36
Maranta leuconeura 36
Mesembryanthemum 46
Monstera deliciosa 25
Nephrolepis acuminata 19
Nephrolepis biserrata 19
Nephrolepis cordifolia 19
Nephrolepis Duffii 19
Nephrolepis ensiformis 19
Nephrolepis exaltata 19
Nephrolepis pectinata 19
Neoregelia 32
Nidularium 32
Old Man Cactus 49
Opuntia Bigelowii 46, 47
Opuntia cylindrica 46
Opuntia diademata 46
Opuntia elata 46
Opuntia Ficus indica 46
Opuntia leucotricha 46
Opuntia microdasys 46
Opuntia tunicata 46, 47
Opuntia vulgaris 46
Orchids 60
Orchis 60
Palms 37–39
Panax 23
Paphiopedilum 62, 63
Paphiopedilum callosum 63
Paphiopedilum insigne 63
Paphiopedilum praestans 63
Paphiopedilum Rothischildianum 63
Paphiopedilum Spicerianum 63
Paphiopedilum Stonei 63
Paphiopedilum villosum 63
Pereskia aculeata 52
Pelargonium crispum 58
Pelargonium domesticum 58
Pelargonium graveolens 58
Pelargonium inquinans 58
Pelargonium odoratissimum 58
Pelargonium peltatum 58
Pelargonium zonale 58
Peperomia argyroneura 27
Peperomia caperata 27
Peperomia griseo-argentea 27
Peperomia marmorata 27
Peperomia obtusifolia 27
Peperomia verschaffeltii 27
Philodendron bipinnatifidum 25
Philodendron erubescens 25
Philodendron pertusum 25
Philodendron scandens 25
Philodendron Selloum 25
Phoenix canariensis 38, 39
Phoenix dactylifera 38, 39
Platycerium 21
Platycerium angolense 21
Platycerium bifurcatum 21
Platycerium coronarium 21
Platycerium grande 21
Platycerium Hillii 21
Platycerium Walchii 21
Platycerium wilhelmina 21
Poinsettia 55
Polypodium glaucophyllum 19
Polyscias fruticosa 23

Polyscias Guilfoylei 23
Polyscias rumphiana 23
Pteridophytes 17
Pteris biaurita 19
Pteris cretica 19
Pteris dentata 19
Pteris tremula 19
Raphis 38, 39
Rochea 41
Rhododendron indicum 59
Rhododendron Kaempferi 59
Rhododendron molle 59
Rhododendron obtusum 59
Rhododendron simsii 59
Rubber plant 28
Saintpaulia diplotricha 56

Saintpaulia ionantha 56
Saintpaulia tongwensis 56
Sansevieria cylindrica 31
Sansevieria hahnii 31
Sansevieria trifasciata 31
Sansevieria zeylanica 31
Schlumbergera 52
Scindapsus aureus 25
Sedum 40, 41
Sedum acre 40
Sedum Adolphii 40
Sedum alpestre 40
Sedum caeruleum 40
Sedum Telphium 40
Sedum album 40
Sedum praealtum 40

Sedum rupestre 40
Sedum Sieboldi 40
Sedum spurium 40
Selaginella apoda 17
Selaginella canaliculata 17
Selaginella caulescens 17
Selaginella denticulata 17
Selaginella Kraussiana 17
Selaginella lepidophylla 17
Selaginella Martensi 17
Selaginella uncinata 17
Selaginella Wildenovii 17
Selenicereus 48
Sempervivum 41
Stanhopea 61
Syagrus Weddelliana 38

Tillandsia 32
Vanda caerulea 61
Vanda insignis 61
Vanda Sanderiana 61
Vanda teres 61
Vriesia 32
Wax plant 57
Zantedeschia aethiopica 54
Zantedeschia albo-maculata 54
Zantedeschia Ellottiana 54
Zantedeschia melanoleuca 54
Zantedeschia Rehmanni 54
Zebra plant 31
Zygocactus 52

Pteridophytes: selaginellas, ferns

Selaginellas

Selaginellas are very small plants that can easily pass unobserved but deserve a closer look because of the elegance of their foliage.

Origins. The genus *Selaginella* belongs to the Selaginellaceae family and has about 700 species distributed throughout the tropics. Some of them can be found on walls and on rocks, or on scanty Alpine pastures, or even in sunny locations (*S. denticulata*). The species are of tropical or subtropical origin and are cultivated for ornamental purposes because of their delicate foliage.

Morphology. They are creeping or erect plants and many of them are moss-like in appearance. The leaves have a spiral arrangement on erect stems, or 3 or 4 rows on prostrate stems. Their size can vary.

Their cultivation demands the shelter of a frame or greenhouse that can be cool, temperate, or warm according to the species. They require a loose and rather acid soil with much organic matter, a humid atmosphere, and diffused light. They are propagated by division.

Species and varieties. Among the species of particular ornamental value are:

Selaginella Martensi comes from Mexico and

1

is among the most widely used species in cultivation. There are many varieties. It has tile-shaped leaves that are bright green and are carried by an erect stem which emerges from a creeping stolon. It is a species for cool temperatures.

S. uncinata requires a warm temperature and is native to China. It has stems that reach 25 inches and green-bluish leaves.

S. canaliculata is from the Himalayas and it is also a warm temperature species. It has bright green branches that may reach 4 feet.

S. Wildenovii is best at cool temperatures and is native to India and the East Indies. It can have stems as long as 20 feet and is vine-like.

S. caulescens, from Japan, is a type upright to a maximum of 12 inches. It is particularly fine in the *argentea* (silver), *amoena* and *Japonica*

varieties.

S. lepidophylla is native to Texas and south to Mexico and Central America. It is a "resurrection" plant, that during periods of drought bends its external branches to form a ball easily carried by the wind; when the humidity increases, the branches stretch out again and the plant starts to grow.

S. Kraussiana, native to South Africa, has a creeping or trailing habit.

---

1. *Selaginella Kraussiana.*

2. Close view of *Selaginella Kraussiana.*

3. *Selaginella apoda.*

2　3

4

5

6

Maidenhair fern

In the semi-tropics or tropics, under conditions of high humidity and diffused light, it is common to find the maidenhair fern (*Adiantum Capillus-Veneris*). This plant has been known since antiquity and has been described by famous naturalists like Dioscoris, Pliny and Theophrastus for for exaggerated therapeutic virtues.

Morphology. The numerous species of *Adiantum* (about 200), a genus of ferns of the Polypodiaceae family, come generally from tropical zones of South America.

They are plants with an elongated rhizome which is covered with dark bracts; the fronds are always delicate and elegant, and can be bipartite, bipinnate, or flagellate. The simple or palmate leaves are almost always glabrous and dark green, tender or greenish blue, or yellowish.

Species and varieties. Many species of *Adiantum* are cultivated because of their ornamental appearance; they are largely used for floral arrangements because of the elegance and delicacy of their foliage.

With the exception of the American Maidenhair (*S. pedatum*), the *Adiantums* must be kept in a cold frame during winter. During the growing period, they prefer half shade with a mild temperature and abundant humidity. The soil must be of a loose texture and suited to hold water. Use a mixture of leaf mould, peat, and loam soil.

They propagate naturally by spores in a humid environment, but are also easily propagated by division of the clumps.

The most widely spread species are: *A. Capillus-Veneris*; *A. tenerum* var. *farleyense*, with elegant forms; *A. rhodophyllum* and *A. rubellum*, that have reddish leaves when young; *A. birkenneadii* with triangular leaves; *A. cuneatum*, light yellow-green coloured and with very delicate branches; *A. trapeziforme*; *A. peruvianum*; and *A. curvatum* with forked fronds.

---

4. Maidenhair of the *Adiantum tenerum* var. *roseum* species.

5. The common Maidenhair fern: *Adiantum Capillus-Veneris*.

6. The delicate foliage of the *Adiantum tenerum* var. *roseum* seen from above.

7

8

Pteris and nephrolepsis

These two genera of ferns belonging to the Polypodiaceae family that have long been known and are easily cultivated as house plants. They are tropical and subtropical in origin.

Pteris. The "P" in the name is not pronounced. The *Pteris* genus has fronds that are attractive, leathery, glabrous or hairy, regular or irregular, pinnate or pluripinnate. Known species number about 250, but only about 30 are cultivated for ornamental purposes.

They need a light, textured soil composed of mixtures of top soils, peat, leaf mould, and sand. They propagate by spores, but division of clumps is much simpler. They are grown in a temperate or warm greenhouse.

P. biaurita, of tropical origin, is very well known in the silver (*argentea*) and *tricolor* varieties for the elegant colouration of the foliage.

P. cretica is a species for cooler temperatures that is widely grown; varieties include *crispata*, *sempervirens* and *albolineata*.

P. dentata, of tropical origin, has leaves as long as 3 feet while those of *P. tremula* may be even longer.

P. ensiformis, with slender fertile fronds up to 20 inches in length, is native to Eastern Asia and Australia.

P. serrulata, native to China and Japan, has slender fronds up to 18 inches; varieties are crested.

P. tremula, known as Australia Brake, has bright green fronds up to 36 inches.

Nephrolepsis. The *Nephrolepsis* genus, also of the Polypodiaceae family, has about 30 species of tropical origin that are considered among the best ferns for house plants because of their elegance and their easy culture.

They have a short stolon-like stem covered with brown, thin fringed scales. The fronds bear pinnate leaves as long as 3 feet.

Reproduction takes place by spores, but it is easiest to divide the plant.

Among the best-known species are:

N. cordifolia, native to Japan and New Zealand. It is a species suited to cool temperatures and is cultivated in numerous forms as *Compacta*, *modulata* and *pluma*.

N. acuminata with the varieties *furcans*, and *multicaps*.

N. Duffii, native to New Zealand and South Sea islands, is small sized but very pretty.

N. exalta, the Ladder Fern, native to the tropics, grows up to 3 feet and has a number of varieties, both plumose and crested.

N. hirsutula is another popular species.

Other important species: *N. exalta*, *N. pectinata*, *N. biserrata*.

7. Close up of *Adiantum Capillus-Veneris*.

8. Close up of *Adiantum tenerum* var. *roseum*.

9. Ferns are much appreciated for attractive foliage: *Polypodium glaucophyllum*.

10. A specimen plant of *Nephrolepsis exaltata* var. *bostoniensis*. Boston Fern.

11. Close up of *Pteris ensiformis* var. *victoriae*.

12. Close up of *Pteris cretica* var. *cristata*.

13

Asplenium

This genus of ferns belongs to the Polypodiaceae family. They have long been cultivated and Spleenwort, a common name, refers to an old medicinal use.

The genus has many species (450 according to some authors, 750 according to others), found from the tropics to the mountains of Europe.

Morphology. They vary from small plants a few inches tall to large ones with leaves over 3 feet long, terrestrial, with a few tropical epiphytic species.

The rhizome is creeping or erect, covered with dark bracts. The various-shaped branches have whole or pinnate leaves, more or less erect or decumbent. Many species are cultivated as house plants or in greenhouses.

Cultivation. They require loose soil with a good supply of organic matter, a good mixture being equal parts peat, loam, leaf-mould and sand. They need humid atmosphere, diffused light, and a moderate temperature. They should be watered freely in summer and moderately in winter.

Hardy species for the garden should be positioned in rockeries and old walls.

Propagation is by division of the clumps or from spores. The procumbent species and varieties are cultivated in hanging pots.

Species and varieties. The most popular species are:

A. Nidus-Avis (Bird's Nest Fern), with a whole, large and waved foliage, light-green in colour.

Native to both Europe and America, with ornamental value are *A. rutamuraria*, a small fern of rocks and of old walls, and *A. trichomanes*, sometimes call Maidenhair Spleenwort, both hardy.

---

13. A greenhouse with ferns: in the centre on the right, a beautiful sample of *Asplium Nidus Avis* (Bird's Nest Fern).

Platycerium

The *Platyceriums* are very decorative. Their name, of Greek origin, means "flat horns" and they are commonly called Stag's Horn Fern.

Origins. Almost all are native to the Far East (Australia, Malacca, Thailand) and some species are native to Western Africa and Peru.

Morphology. In their original habitat, the *Platyceriums* live as an epiphyte on trees getting the necessary nutrients by means of particular sterile leaves tightly inserted on a short rhizome that adheres to the trunk with many roots.

The fertile leaves are flattened and dichotomously divided, with an entire margin greyish-green, often pubescent. The sporangia are on the underside along the tips and margins.

Cultivation. The *Platyceriums* are species suited for hothouses and grow well in a mixture of well decomposed soil, sphagnum, and peat, in baskets, or even better, in old tree-trunks hanging from the walls. They need reduced light and uniform humidity. Propagation takes place by spores, which can be sown in pots in a very light soil. They can also easily be multiplied by the young little plants that develop from root buds.

They do not need any special care and live for a long time. If they are taken inside houses, it is necessary to place them in the right light and to provide the necessary humidity.

Species and varieties. The most famous and most decorative species to be considered is *P. bifurcatum*, commonly called Stag's Horn Fern because of the characteristic resemblance.

---

14. *Platycerium bifurcatum* on an old piece of cork.

15. Close up of *P. bifurcatum* with spore bearing leaf.

16. Close up of "flat horns" of the *P. bifurcatum*.

17. Young specimen of *P. angolense*.

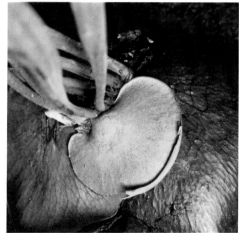
15

14

16   17

Foliage plants

Aspidistra

The Aspidistra is a common plant, once very popular in every home. It is out of style—being associated with the Victorian era.

Origins. It is native to the Far East (Japan, China) and was imported in the early part of nineteenth century. It has created enthusiasm on account of its easy culture and its sturdiness, especially in Britain where it was formerly the most common indoor plant.

The aspidistra was at the height of its popularity among the working and lower middle classes in Britain during the first 30 years of the present century. For a time it became a symbol of respectability and was given this status by George Orwell in his novel "Keep the Aspidistra Flying". Perhaps this arose because the plant was cheap to buy, did not call for any knowledge of gardening from the owner to keep it alive (being resistant to poor conditions and to neglect), and looked imposing by itself in an ornamental pot.

Morphology. The *Aspidistra* genus belong to the Liliaceae family. It has few species of which *A. elatior* is the best known. *Aspidistra* plants are herbaceous, rhizomatous, with numerous acaulous, large, persistent leaves, oblong-lanceolate, leathery, dark green, and striped with white in some cultivars. The bell-shaped flowers are blue or bluish-violet, almost sessile, not ornamental and are a scientific curiosity since they have, contrary to the Liliaceae in general, 8 stamens and an ovary with 4 locules. The fruit is a globose berry with numerous seeds.

Cultivation. Chiefly kept indoors and only used as a foliage plant. Very resistant to the worst conditions of humidity, dust and light, it will also tolerate frost. It can therefore be used in regions with a mild climate outdoors, where it is suitable for thickets and borders in cool and shaded areas of the garden. It is very vigorous and grows in any type of soil. Propagation is performed in spring by division of the clumps, with the precaution that each piece of rhizome must bear at least one leaf. The single segments are planted 3 or 4 per pot and new root development is favoured in warm conditions.

Species and varieties. The species of chief interest is the *A. elatior*, also known as the Parlour Palm. It grows up to 2 feet, and the variety *variegata* has leaves striped cream.

Garden varieties are not well classified. They are distinguished by the different colour of the leaves that appear variegated or dotted.

---

18. The traditional *Aspidistra elatior* with its large, shiny leaves.

19. *Fatsia japonica*, sometimes incorrectly called *Aralia japonica* var. *sieboldii*.

20. *Fatsia japonica* var. *Moseri*.

21. A branch of *Fatshedera Lizei*.

18

20   21

22

23

24

Aralias

This name has been given to several plants that botanically now belong to different genera such as *Fatsia*, *Dizygotheca*, *Panax*, *Polyscias*, and others. Considering the nature of the present volume, it is inadvisable to get involved in the morphological differences; the space can be given more profitability to a brief consideration of those species that are of interest from the ornamental gardening point of view. These genera belong to the Araliaceae family. They were introduced into Britain in the mid-seventeenth century.

Morphology. Their appearance is shrubby or like small trees with palmate, compound digitate leaves that are almost linear in some forms or whole. The inflorescence is globose, mostly umbrella-shape, with tiny flowers of no ornamental value. The fruit is a berry.

When cultivated they are used for decorating houses and offices, where, if given attention, they last a long time. They can also be used in groups for temporary decoration of gardens during the summer season.

Cultivation. They are propagated by seed or by cuttings, and even by grafting and layering.

They are plants suited to a temperate greenhouse with an optimum around 58°F. They grow best in a diffused light. As far as the soil is concerned, they are not demanding, but a good soil mixture should include leaf mould, top soil and sand. Irrigation should be frequent, but not abundant; the soil should be well-drained.

Species and varieties. *A. chinensis*, the Chinese Angelica Tree, grows to 20 feet. *A. elara*, the Japanese Angelica Tree, grows to 35 feet. *A. nudicaulis*, native to North America, up to 4 feet, is known as the Wild Sarsaparilla.

Fatsia japonica is a widely dispersed tree, very popular for the elegance of its large leaves, particularly charming in the *variegata* variety, spotted with yellow or white. Propagation is by seed or by cuttings.

Dizygotheca elegantissima is a plant worthy of its name because of the light beauty of its leaves that are thin and waxy. It is generally propagated by grafting on *Fatsia japonica* or *Oreopanax reticulatum*, or by cuttings, under glass.

Polyscias fruticosa with the *plumata* variety; *P. Guilfoylei*, with the *laciniata*, *Victoria* and *montrosa* varieties; and *P. rumphiana* are pretty house plants even though they are not as well known as the *Fatsia*.

Fatshedera Lizei is a hybrid between the *Fatsia* and *Hedera*. It is evergreen, tolerates indoor conditions, and deserves even greater use since it is easy to cultivate and has attractive foliage. *A. spinosa* is the Devil's Walking Stick.

---

22. The lacy appearance of the leaves of *Dizygotheca elegantissima*.

23. Close up of leaves of *Dizygotheca*.

24. *Fatsia japonica*, a young seedling.

25

26

27

28

29

Asparagus

The name certainly brings to our mind the memory of delicious dishes that gourmets prepare in various ways for the joy of food lovers. Here we omit the edible species that are only used for the table in order to call attention to those cultivated as greenhouse and house plants.

Origins. These plants are of different origins: some species are from the Mediterranean region; some come from Siberia, the Orient, and from South Africa.

The *Asparagus* genus belongs to the Liliaceae family and includes about 300 species.

Morphology. They are all perennial herbaceous plants, with fleshy roots and runners or climbing stems. Many small branches, whose configurations and development vary with each species, function as leaves. The axillary or terminal flowers are arranged in racemes and are small. The fruit is a berry containing globose and flattened seeds.

Cultivation. Omitting the common garden asparagus, numerous other species are culti-

vated in greenhouses, both for the elegant decorative effect they provide when set in pots and as a source of foliage which can be cut for floral arrangements. They are easy to grow and can be propagated by seeds or by division. They are tolerant as far as the soil is concerned, but they are injured by cold.

Species and varieties. The species grown as ornamentals are:

A. verticillatus, used for covering walls and fences.

A. Sprengeri, with needle-like drooping foliage.

A. asparagoides, used by florists especially in the myrtifolius cultivated variety.

A. plumosus (Asparagus fern), with the cultivars *tenuissimus, compactus, nanus* and others is the most used species for floral decorations.

---

25. Note the airiness of the *Asparagus plumosus* var. *nanus.*

26. Close up of *Asparagus plumosus.*

Philodendron

The Greek roots of the name (*phileo* = to love and *dendron* = tree) describes the natural habit of this clinging vine.

Origins. Native to tropical forests of South America, *Philodendrons* are typical plants of the undergrowth from which they emerge attaching themselves to taller trees by their adventitious roots. Introduced in cultivation more than a century ago, they are cultivated for the beauty of their leaves and for the elegant appearance that makes them desirable for greenhouses and houses.

The *Philodendrons* are Monocotyledons belonging to the family of the Araceae. The number of the classified species is controversial, but according to recent studies is close to 100.

31

Morphology. Herbaceous and vining plants, they have a thick stem with long internodes and are provided with numerous and thick aerial roots. The leaves are large, often very large, shiny, and leathery. The shape of the leaves is variable, and can be cordate, oval, sagittate, or pole-shaped, with entire, lobate, or pinnate margins. The flowers (blossoms develop in greenhouses on large specimens) are unisexual, gathered into a spadix inflorescence wrapped by a gaudy spathe that is creamy-white, pinkish or yellowish. The single fruits are fleshy berries.

Cultivation. The *Philodendrons* are plants with great ornamental value, both for house and

32

greenhouse, and their use continues to increase. Their cultivation in greenhouses with a high humidity is very easy. They are grown in pots according to the plant size and ultimate use. The soil may be a mixture of loam, organic matter, and sand.

They prefer diffused light and it is best to avoid strong or cold draughts. The propagation is by cuttings, and roots develop in a warm humid environment. Layering is also possible but it is done less frequently. Tip cuttings obtained from the apex make the most attractive plants.

Species and varieties. The species of *Philodendrons* and the cultivars are many. Among the familiar ones is *P. scandens* (Sweetheart Vine), well-known for its tolerance to indoor conditions, with its varieties *variegatum* and *aureovariegatum*.

Also worthy of mention are: *P. Selloum*, with large, oval, oblong leaves; *P. bipinnatifidum*, that is bushy and not climbing; *P. erubescens*, admired for the oval shape and the pink undercolour of the leaves.

Other species cultivated include *P. Andreanum*, that has flowers wrapped in a gaudy spathe of black, purple and creamy white, and *P. verrucosum* (syn. *P. Lindenii*) of dwarf habit. *P. giganteum* has broad heart-shaped leaves.

The *Monstera deliciosa* belongs to the Araceae and can commonly be mistaken for *Philodendron pertusum*. It has an equally decorative value and similar culture.

34

27. Fruits of *Asparagus Sprengeri*.

28. *Monstera deliciosa*, in hydroponic culture.

29. Related to the *Philodendrons* is the *Scindapsus aureus*, cultivar "Marble Queen".

30, 31. A popular house plant is *Philodendron scandens* with the elegant, heart-shaped leaves emphasized in the illustration.

32. Cutting of *Philodendron scandens*; the actual roots coming out of the node are evident.

33. A nice specimen of *Philodendron Selloum*.

34. *Monstera deliciosa*, pretty plant of the Araceae family, adhering to the stone wall of a greenhouse.

33

35

38

36

39

40

Begonias

A whole volume could be written on these popular plants that are well known for the beauty of their leaves, the grace and abundance of their blooms, and the variability in shapes—qualities that make them excellent plants for house decoration, gardens, and for long-lasting flower beds.

Origins. All species of the *Begonia* genus that are cultivated originated in the American and Asiatic tropics, from where they were imported to Europe first in 1770. A few, like the *B. veitchii*, came from the Andes at more than 13,000 feet.

It is the most important genus of the Begoniaceae family, to which it gives its name. The number of species is controversial, but there are probably more than 500.

Morphology. These are herbaceous or slightly shrubby plants with a succulent appearance. Their stem can be extensively branched or reduced to a rhizome, to a tuber, or to a bulb-like tuber. The leaves are stalked, alternate, and often asymmetric; they are of various shapes including orbicular, reniform, peltate and palmate; they can also be bristly, especially on the underside, with a whole or toothed margin. Almost all species have leaves with beautiful colours that include all variations of green, from a light to a very dark shade, with metallic reflections, or purple of different intensity and with variegations and designs of interesting effect. The sexual flowers are very small in some species, but abundant; in others, they are large and showy, in white, pink, red or yellow. The fruits are winged capsules with many tiny seeds.

Cultivation. The cultivation of begonias is not difficult and, although there are differences according to the species, the soil, light, temperature, and water requirements are common to all.

The basis for a good begonia cultivation is provided by an environment that is warm and humid, and in which the plants receive diffused light, soil rich in organic matter or peat, or leaf mould and sand, and abundant watering.

Begonias are propagated by seed and by cuttings of a branch or a leaf, or even, in some species, by division of the rhizomes or of the tubers. Seed is used for *Begonia semperflorens*, the well-known everblooming begonia used for flower beds and borders. Seed is planted in autumn or in spring, in pots under glass and without covering. The seedlings must be transplanted.

The cutting of a leaf or a shoot is commonly used because of the ability of begonias to regenerate tissues easily; the cuttings, when rooted, accurately reproduce the mother plant. Propagation by division of rhizomes and tubers is peculiar to a few species, such as *B. tuberhybrida*.

Species and varieties. Due to lack of space, attention is called to only a few of the most common species.

B. albo-picta is cultivated for its glossy green ornamental leaves spotted with silver, flowers are greenish-white. *B. argenteo-guttata*, another species grown for the beauty of its leaves, has foliage speckled with white, and is a hybrid growing to 4 feet.

B. semperflorens, or garden begonia, is used in borders, flower beds, carpet bedding, and for pot plants. Cultivars include Linda, Scarletta, Matador, Pink Pearl, Viva and Indian Maid.

B. tuberhybrida is the well-known tuberous begonia that embellishes terraces and grows well even in semi-shaded flower beds, producing a bloom with warm and luminous shades from June to November, in numerous varieties with single and double flowers that may be erect or pendulous, cristate, or fringed. Seed of these is sold by flower colour or as a mixture.

B. Rex, *B. asplenifolia*, *B. metallica* and *B. socotrana* ("Gloire de Lorraine") are all cultivated for their magnificent foliage, as are *B. alleryi*, a hybrid that grows to 4 feet; *B. heracleifolia* that has deeply lobed foliage; and *B. imperialis* with foliage both deep velvety and bright green.

---

35. The beautiful, variegated foliage of the *Begonia Rex*, cultivar "Iron Cross".

36. Young potted plant of *Begonia semperflorens*, cultivar "Vernon".

37-38 Flowers of *Begonia tuberhybrida*, the bulbous begonia.

39. Single flower of *Begonia*, cultivar "Vernon".

40. *Begonia Scharffii* (syn. *B. haegeana*) flowers.

42

41. *Peperomia caperata* in flower.

42. Leaf cutting of *Peperomia caperata* with a sprout; on the right, a leaf cutting just made.

43. Pot with *Peperomia caperata*.

44. *Peperomia griseo argentea*.

45. Leaf cutting of *Peperomia griseo argentea*.

41

43

44

45

Peperomias

These plants, native to tropical regions (Brazil, Peru, Argentina), were introduced in the second half of the nineteenth century.

The genus *Peperomia* belongs to the Piperaceae family. Its name means "pepper-like" indicating a certain similarity with the genus, *Piper*. There are about 100 species.

Morphology. They are evergreen herbaceous plants, with a radical leaf arrangement and a short stem that is barely developed; the alternate fleshy leaves are opposite or verticillate, have an entire margin, cordiform or rounded acuminate, and frequently have interesting variegations. Peculiar and interesting are the clustered in-

florescences that look like "mouse tails", with a white cream colour. The flowers are insignificant as far as decoration is concerned, and the same is true for the fruits that are little berries with thin pericarps.

Cultivation. The decorative value of the leaves, the ease of cultivation in the greenhouse, and their long life in the house make peperomias much appreciated. The small size and the modest development of the plant suggests cultivation in little pots with a soil mixture of loam, peat or organic matter, and sand. To get good results, it is necessary to provide a shaded location and to avoid excessive watering.

Peperomias can be propagated by seed which should be scattered in pots, in fine, loose soil. Usually, however, the plants are propagated by cuttings in spring. The little segments of stems with a leaf are placed in sand in a propagation greenhouse or frame; they will need to be constantly shaded and watered.

Species and varieties. Among the most popular peperomias are: *Peperomia obtusifolia*, with green leaves and marginal dark spots; *P. marmorata* and *P. verschaffeltii*, with green, marbled leaves; *P. argyroneura*, with green leaves and silver stripes; *P. caperata*, with green and fleshy leaves.

46

47

48

49

Rubber plants

The *Ficus* are among the most well known, widely used and best loved of house plants. Their popularity is certainly derived from the decorativeness of the plant whose leaves, although somewhat stiff, are nonetheless beautiful.

Origins. The *Ficus* are native to Central and South America and Asia. Those most commonly cultivated as decorative plants have been imported from India and Malaysia.

The *Ficus* belong to the Moraceae family and include more than 600 species.

Morphology. They can be trees, or shrubby, herbaceous and climbing plants. The tall *Ficus* often have aerial adventitious roots that grow to the ground forming a colonnade around the main stem. Others have long flat roots shaped like supports around the plant. Their leaves are lobate or entire, plain or wavy, alternate and almost always persistent, leathery, with clearly-marked veins. Sometimes different leaf shapes are found in the same plant. The width of the leaves varies from species to species and in them stipules that cover the terminal buds are always present.

Ficus are mainly monoecious plants, with a characteristic inflorescence shaped like a swollen axis that is fleshy, concave and composed of unisexual sessile flowers. The fruits are achenes. All *Ficus* secrete a white latex that is thick and often caustic.

The Biblical fig tree (*Ficus Sycomorous*) and the common fig (*Ficus carica*) are used for their fruit. Others produce types of latex used for making lacquers.

Cultivation. These plants are propagated in a hot and shaded greenhouse with an optimal temperature around 65°F and high humidity. They can be propagated by tip cuttings or stem cuttings. The cuttings root in a warm, moist environment. Once the roots have taken, pot the cuttings in fertile and loose soil composed of three parts of organic matter, two parts of top soil, and one part of sand.

Species and varieties. The most popular species is *F. elastica* (Indian Rubber Plant) and its cultivar *decora*, which has dark green, rigid, oblong, lanceolate leaves enclosed in the bud by a red sheath.

F. lyrata is a pretty plant, commonly called Fiddleleaf Fig because of the characteristic shape of the leaves that look like a violin and may reach 15 inches in length.

Worthy of mention is *F. diversifolia* (Mistletoe Fig), that demonstrates heterophylly and bears at the axil of the leaves numerous yellow berries.

F. radicans variegata, has leaves variegated with silver. *F. rubiginosa*, native to Australia, has leaves with a rusty appearance underneath (also known as *F. australis*).

Finally, the *F. pumila* (Creeping Fig), more commonly known as *F. repens*, has a climbing stem and is suitable for covering an entire wall in a greenhouse; it has small, leathery leaves which are heterophyllous on the terminal flowering branches.

50

51

52

53

54

55

Dracaenas

These plants have been introduced from tropical Africa, from islands of the Indian Ocean, and from Central America. Some are extremely elegant in their habit of growth and attractive foliage. They are very suitable for house decoration, although they have rather exacting temperature and atmospheric requirements.

They are monocotyledeons belonging to the Liliaceae family and the genus *Dracaena* has about 40 species, half of which are of interest to the horticulturalist. They were introduced into Britain in the early seventeenth century.

---

46. Cuttings of *Ficus* on the bench of a propagation greenhouse.

47. *Ficus repens*: in the foreground a fertile branch presenting the phenomenon of heterophylly (leaves of different shapes).

48. *Ficus repens* on the wall of a greenhouse.

49. *Ficus elastica*: the cutting has originated a new plant.

50. *F. pandurata*.

51. *Dracaena Draco*: young plant in a pot.

52. *Cordyline indivisa*, formerly known as *Dracaena indivisa*.

53. *Dracaena deremensis* var. *Warneckii*.

54. Young tip cutting of *Dracaena deremensis*.

55. Group of *Dracaena arborea*.

Morphology. These shrubby plants become trees on maturity. The cultivated species develop at a moderate rate, and have a rigid and erect stem which is covered with long, sessile or largely-stalked, ensiform or ovate, lanceolate or elliptical leaves. The leaves are an attractive green and may be uniform or striped with white. The inflorescences are numerous in a head or a cluster, composed of small single flowers having a whitish-green or yellowish-green colour, and are of only little value ornamentally. The fruit is a berry with three ovules.

Until 1868, the year in which it was destroyed by a violent storm, a specimen of *Dracaena Draco*, uprooted in Tenerife, was considered to be one of the largest trees (measuring 46 feet in circumference) and one of the oldest (the age was estimated at 6,000 years). From trees of this species in their native countries, a resin is obtained that is used in the preparation of varnishes and lacquers, as a modifier in synthetic plastics, and for therapeutic purposes.

Cultivation. *Dracaenas* are greatly appreciated for their ornamental qualities and have established themselves in a favourable position among the various ornamental indoor plants.

They are cultivated in a temperate or warm greenhouse at from 55 to 60°F. They may be reproduced from seed but are more commonly propagated by cuttings or by air layering. They grow best in a light fertile soil, that can be made of one part peat and one part loam, mixed with one-half part sand.

Species and varieties. Among the most cultivated species, the following are especially fine: *Dracaena deremensis* is particularly attractive, with graceful green leaves striped with silver. Its variety, *Bausei* has a leaf wholly silver and a silvery stem.

D. Draco, native to the Canary Islands, is known as the Dragon Tree and has glaucous leaves. It is hardy along the maritime areas of Devon and Cornwall and in the Scilly Isles.

D. parrii is hardy and can be grown outside in summer. For this reason it is a favourite for bedding displays and is used by gardeners of country houses and municipal parks.

Named after orchid expert Henry Sander, the species *D. sanderi* has thin, slightly wavy leaves rarely exceeding one inch across. The centre of the leaf is a greyish green with a few lines of ivory.

Also worthy of note are: *D. fragans* in the varieties *Lindenii* and *Massangeana*; *D. Hookeriana*; *D. Goldieana*; and *D. Godseffiana*, appreciated for its shrubby appearance and its dark green spiraled leaves which are spotted in a light colour. The latter was named after Joseph Godseff, a well-known gardener and plant collector of the early years of the present century. A cultivar, Florida Beauty, has leaves spotted with cream and is a very showy plant.

Finally, two beautiful species that belong to the genus *Cordyline*, but which are commonly called dracaenas; they are fine plants with brightly coloured leaves and are named *Cordyline terminalis* and *Cordyline indivisa*, with long and narrow leaves and elegant appearance.

56

57

58

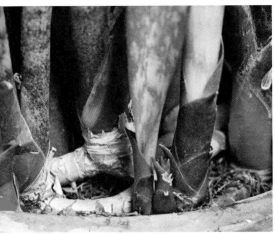

59

60

61

62

Sansevierias

Dedicated to Raymond of Sangrio, Prince of Sansevero, this genus contains some of the most widely-used species for indoor decoration.

Popular names for the genus are Bowstring Hemp or Angola Hemp.

Origins. Sansevierias originated in regions of tropical and subtropical Africa, India and Ceylon. They were introduced into Britain in the seventeenth century. The genus belongs to the Liliaceae family.

Morphology. These are perennial herbaceous plants (a few species are woody); they grow in clumps and have a thick and short rhizome from

which a very short stem develops. The leaves, which represent a large part of the plant, are thick, leathery and fibrous. They range in length from a very few inches to 3 feet, have flat or slightly concave sides that are also ensiform, and are grey-greenish or green, and spotted or striped with clear transversal lines. A few species have cylindrical and very peculiar leaves. The flowers, carried by long scapes in a large number, are in clusters and have a tubular shape with a perianth of 6 greenish-white petals; they are strongly scented, but do not have any ornamental value.

In their native countries they are grown for the strong fibre from their leaves which is suitable for the weaving of ropes.

Cultivation. The cultivation of sansevierias is done in temperate greenhouses. The soil of the pots should be rather heavy; it is formed by mixing one part loam and one part organic matter with one-half part sand. It is necessary to control the temperature, which must never go below 45 to 50°F (at 43° sansevierias are injured). They do not need particular care. Moderate waterings must be given in winter. In summer they can be located in warm and well-lighted locations.

The plant seems to thrive on neglect and if not repotted will continue to flourish. Some experts believe it prefers to be pot-bound and that the right time to repot the plant is when its roots

63

64

Aphelandras (Zebra plants)

Aphelandras are attractive both for their leaves and for their flowers, and so should always find a place in the greenhouse. They were imported more than a century ago from Mexico and Brazil.

Morphology. Because of the stripes on their leaves, they have also been called "zebra plants". Aphelandras are evergreen, shrubby or herbaceous and sturdy plants, belonging to the Acanthaceae family and included in the genus *Aphelandra*. There are about 80 species of which about 10 are of interest for decoration.

They have opposite, simple, ovate-lanceolate, rigid, pinnate-veined leaves that have a bright green colour striped with white or yellow; the underside is often reddish. The inflorescence is an erect, terminal cluster with a characteristic pyramidal shape and has "tiled" bracts that are red or yellow. The single flowers are sessile, bilabiate, and tubular and display different colours: yellow, red, orange. The fruit is a dehiscent capsule containing 4 seeds.

Cultivation. Aphelandras, in recent years, have emerged from their role as botanical peculiarities and have proved to be excellent house plants. They reproduce by seed and are easily propagated by cuttings of young shoots. They are demanding as far as the soil is concerned because they prefer a well-fertilized soil with well-decomposed organic matter.

A good mixture is made up of 2 parts loam, $1\frac{1}{2}$ parts leaf mould, 1 part cow manure, $\frac{1}{2}$ part sharp sand plus bonemeal.

They are cultivated in a warm greenhouse (only a few species, like the *Aphelandra aurantiaca*, can adjust itself to a temperate greenhouse) at 72 to 77°F with high humidity. After blooming, for a period of rest, they are placed in a 41 to 43°F environment, and their watering is limited. They should be repotted yearly.

Species and varieties. The most commonly-cultivated aphelandras belong to the species *A. squarrosa*, with green shiny leaves having veins emphasized by white and yellow stripes; the inflorescence has bracts and flowers in the same dark yellow colour. The cultivar *Louisae* is one of the best pot plants.

The *A. aurantiaca*, hardier in regard to temperature requirements, has a duller and uniform green colour, and an orange inflorescence. Interesting also are *A. fascinator* and *A. tetragona*, which are shrubby and very pretty species with scarlet inflorescences.

A. pectinata, native to South America, grows to 3 feet and has vivid scarlet inflorescences.

actually crack the pot it is in. The foliage needs to be kept clean.

Propagation is by division of the clumps, in spring. It is also possible to use a leaf cutting, but the characteristic variegation is not retained. The thick clumps should be repotted every year, toward the end of spring, using a pot that is larger than the previous one; a good liquid fertilization will favour the growth of new leaves.

Species and varieties. The most widely-spread species is *Sansevieria zeylanica*, correctly known as *S. trifasciata*, of which the *laurentii* variety, with green leaves that are grey-striped and have yellow edges, is the most beautiful.

The *S. hahnii*, Birds' Nest Sansevieria, is rather short and has rosette leaves; and the *S. cylindrica* species has cylindrical leaves.

S. thyrsiflora (also known as *S. guineensis*) grows up to 18 inches, and has leaves banded pale green and greenish-white flowers. It is native to South Africa.

56. The small and pretty *Sansevieria hahnii* in the pot.

57. Young sprouts of *Sansevieria hahnii*.

58. Sprout of *Sansevieria* originated by a cutting.

59. Close up of the rhizome of *Sansevieria trifasciata*.

60. *Sansevieria hahnii*.

61. *Sansevieria trifasciata* var. *Laurentii* in hydroponic culture.

62. Leaf cuttings of *Sansevieria trifasciata* var. *Laurentii*.

63-64. The attractive leaves of the *Aphelandra squarrosa*.

65 66 67

Aechmeas

These very elegant plants are undoubtedly destined to increase in popularity and to be incorporated more frequently in interior decorating schemes.

Origins. The *Aechmeas* are plants characteristic of the tropical and subtropical flora of South America and have become the most popular of all bromelaids.

The *Aechmea* genus belongs to the Bromeliaceae family, that provides numerous greenhouse and house plants. The most famous representative of the family is *Ananas comosus*, the pineapple.

The *Aechmea* species includes about 60 known members, only a few of which are cultivated. However, there is an ever-growing number of hybrids.

Morphology. The *Aechmeas* attract attention for their rigid, opened, spiny, and curved leaves, which are marbled or striped with white, and are sometimes pinkish on the lower surface. The inflorescence, a cluster located in the centre of the rosette of leaves, has single flowers in the axil of coloured bracts. The fruit are fleshy, ornamental berries.

Cultivation. Exclusively cultivated for the indoors, these plants have stimulated the flower growers' interest. Cultivation is in a temperate greenhouse, in a small pot, since the root development of the *Aechmeas* is small. This plant demands the use of a particularly suitable soil medium that can be made of, for example, three part organic matter, one-half part of sand and sphagnum, and one part of good top soil.

Propagation may be by seed, but it is preferable to utilize the shoots that form at the base of the plant. The best time to divide is late spring. The shoots are potted and kept at 80 to 85°F until the roots take. The adult plants require a temperate greenhouse, abundant but indirect light, and frequent watering.

Species and varieties. The most cultivated species of *Aechmeas* are *A. fasciata* with dark blue flowers and bracts, and *A. fulgens*, with longer leaves and purple flowers with scarlet sepals.

A. Barleei, native to the West Indies, has yellow flowers and grows up to 2 feet; *A. coelestis* from Brazil has blue flowers; *A. Drakeana*, rose and blue flowers, from Ecuador, grows to 18 inches.

Other Bromeliaceae. Very close systematically to the *Aechmeas*, and often confused with them, are other genera of Bromeliaceae that are of interest for the beauty of their leaves and flowers. Examples: *Billbergia, Vriesia, Tillandsia, Nidularium, Cryptanthus, Neoregelia, Gusmania*.

---

65. *Aechmea fulgens* with its elegant foliage and beautiful inflorescence.

66. Another pretty *Aechmea*.

67. Flower of *Aechmea*.

68, 69. Very similar to the *Aechmea* are other Bromeliaceae such as the *Neoregelia* (68) and the *Gusmania* (69).

68 69

70

Caladium

The elegant shape of the leaves and the variety of colours which they display place these plants among those most commonly used in the greenhouse and in houses, where they bestow a note of marked refinement even though they do not last for a long time.

Origins. The *Caladium* originate in the warm humid forests of Brazil, where they grow naturally as part of the undergrowth in woods along the rivers and streams. They were introduced in Europe in the second half of the eighteenth century and have since attracted great interest among floriculturists. A great deal of attention has been focused on them by the general public at flower shows.

Caladium is a genus of the Araceae family that includes peculiar and interesting plants. It has many species and numerous hybrids.

Morphology. They are herbacious plants with a tuberous rhizome from which the leaves develop. The leaves have long stalks, are mostly sagittate or sagittate-cordate shape but can even be eliptical-ovate, and are as large as 24 inches with evident veins. The colours, which make the leaves extremely beautiful, vary from pink to crimson to red and are concentrated in the centre with the margin remaining more or less marbled or dotted.

The spadix inflorescence is wrapped by a white spathe and is scented. The fruits are whitish berries, that fall on reaching maturity.

Cultivation. The cultivation of the *Caladium* is successful if one creates the conditions characteristic of their original habitat. The pots are carried dry over winter at a temperature of about 60°F. Between January and April, the soil around the tuber is cleaned off and the young buds that are not yet developed are planted in a mixture of leaf mould, top soil, and sand, and then placed in the greenhouse at 65 to 70°F, heavily watered. Once the development of the first leaf has taken place, each young plant will need to be potted; the young plants must be kept in a shaded greenhouse and well supplied with water. In September, waterings will become less frequent until the beginning of the plant's dormant period that will be apparent by the fall of the leaves.

Propagation can take place by means of the little tubers. The *Caladium* are also reproduced by seeds; in this case, the colours of the leaves will appear after the fifth or sixth leaf develops.

Species and varieties. The best-known and most widely-grown species is the *Caladium bicolor*, with bright red leaves in the centre and green around the borders.

Also well known are *C. picturatum* and *C. Schomburgkii*, including numerous cultivars.

Much smaller in size, with ovate, oblong, green-spotted leaves is *C. Humboldtii*. *C. marmoratum* from tropical America grows to 1 foot.

---

70. Beautiful and flashy leaves of *Caladium bicolor*.

71. Note the variation in the leaves of different cultivars of *Caladium*.

Croton

Here are the plants commonly called Crotons; they have colourful foliage and are cultivated in greenhouses for decoration indoors. Botanically they belong to the genus *Codiaeum* and are appreciated both for the bright colours of their leaves and for variations of leaf shape.

Origins. Originating in Malaysian islands, they were imported in the nineteenth century, and since that time have aroused vivid interest and promoted intense activity in selection and hybridization.

The *Codiaeum* genus belongs to the Euphorbiaceae family. Six species are known of which only *Codiaeum variegatum* is interesting to the gardener.

Morphology. These small trees or shrubby plants have persistent, alternate, simple leaves with an entire or lobate margin which demonstrate bright and changeable colours. When the plants are young, the leaves are green and yellow; when the plants mature, red may be the main leaf colour, although the entire range of shades of yellow, orange and red may be included in different combinations. The unisexual flowers, in an axillary raceme, are of little ornamental value.

Cultivation. In their original habitat, the *Codiaeum* grow easily, developing until they form thick and strong bushes. They are referred to as "variegated laurel" by the British. They are exclusively plants for the hot and humid greenhouse, and require a winter temperature of from 65 to 68°F. In frost-free areas, they grow outdoors. They need abundant, but diffused, light and high humidity.

The soil is important for maintaining the plant in the best condition. We suggest a mixture of four parts organic matter, one part good top soil, and one-half part sand.

Propagation is by cuttings. Layering is also used especially to rejuvenate old plants that have been deprived of leaves at the base. The cuttings, taken during the winter and spring, are rooted in sand, and then potted.

Species and varieties. The chief species with a garden interest is *C. variegatum*. The garden varieties are numerous and can be separated into two categories: those with entire leaves and those with lobate leaves. Varieties of *C. variegatum* include *Andreanum* with broad yellow leaves; *Bergmanii*, broad creamy-yellow leaves blotched with green; *Chelsonii*, orange, red and crimson; *Johannis*, green and yellow; *Laingrii*, green, red and salmon; *Weismanni*, green, crimson and magenta; *Evansianum*, green, yellow, crimson and scarlet; *Hawkeri*, creamy white and green; *picturatum*, green, yellow and red; *tricolor*, green, golden yellow and cream; *Warrenii*, striking with green and orange-carmine leaves; *Williamsii*, green, crimson and magenta; and *illustre*, green and yellow leaves.

---

72. Among the prettiest house plants, the *Codiaeum*, commonly named *Croton*, cultivar "Clipper".

73. *Codiaeum variegatum* var. *contorta*, with spiraled leaves.

72

Dieffenbachia

This plant is named in honour of J. F. Dieffenbach, a German botanist who was for many years, around 1830, the supervisor of the castle of Schönbrunn. The plant is a native of tropical America (Brazil, Venezuela, Ecuador and Columbia). In Britain the plant is commonly known as Dumb Cane.

The genus *Dieffenbachia* includes about 12 species and belongs to the Araceae family that includes many other foliage plants (*Philodendron*, *Caladium*, etc.) which are valuable because of the beauty of their leaves.

Morphology. They are herbaceous, shrubby plants with a creeping or erect, succulent stem. The leaves are carried by long semi-cylindrical stalks that are encased for half of their length by a sheath. The leaves are large with an oblong shape, and are basically green, but show a variable degree of spotting or marbling in yellow or grey-green; they have prominent veins. The inflorescence is a spadix with an oblong and persistent spathe and does not have any special ornamental value. The sap is toxic and must not touch mouth or eyes.

Cultivation. As has been mentioned, these plants are of great interest because of the beauty of their leaves and are much used for interior decoration. They have a tendency to lose their basal leaves after months indoors.

Their cultivation demands temperatures around 65 to 68°F, a high humidity, and the avoidance of frequent changes in temperature.

They can be propagated by seed, but are usually propagated by cutting or layers, made in the greenhouse from February to March. The soil used must be loose and light textured and can be of a mixture of three parts organic matter and one part top soil with a little bit of sand.

At the beginning of spring each year, the plants are repotted.

Once they are taken into the house, be sure to place the plants under diffused light in as cool a location as possible.

Species and varieties. There are several garden varieties available on the market; two are *Dieffenbachia picta* and *D. Seguine*. The former has leaves green, white and yellow, and its variety *Jenmannii* has leaves veined and spotted with white, while another variety, *magnifica*, has leaves spotted along the veins.

D. Seguine has leaves green and white. Its three varieties, *irrorata*, *liturata* and *nobilis* are less well-known.

Other commercially grown species are:

D. Bausei, leaves yellowish green blotched dark green and spotted white.

D. Bowmannii, leaves blotched dark and light green, a native of Japan.

D. Carderi, from Colombia, with variegated leaves.

D. Chelsonii, also from Colombia, with leaves green and yellow.

D. Regina, native to South America, has white and green foliage.

74-75. Two varieties of *Dieffenbachia picta*: *arvida* (74) and *superba* (75).

74

75

Calatheas and marantas

The beauty of nature can be admired in a sunset over the sea, in an alpine landscape, or even more simply by observing the delicate embroidery on the leaves of these very pretty plants.

Origins. Both are native to tropical regions of South America, and are located along the large rivers. They have proved themselves to be excellent house plants, especially for large indoor displays.

The *Calathea* and *Maranta* genera both belong to the *Marantaceae* family.

Morphology. They are perennial herbaceous plants that are rhizomatous and are either almost deprived of aerial stems or have a very short one, as in the case of *Maranta*.

The leaves, large in *Calatheas* and smaller in *Marantas*, are on long stalks with a green background, and are variously shaped and coloured, or have very bright and regular stripes. The lower surface is almost always uniformly reddish or it reproduces, in different shades, the same design that is on the upper surface. The flower and the fruit are necessary to make the botanical identification, but do not have any ornamental value.

If we exclude *Maranta arundinacea* that is cultivated in India and Oceania, but mainly in Central America for arrowroot starch, the other species are popular both as greenhouse and house plants, and for gardens in the tropics.

Cultivation. They are warm temperature plants that almost all require a 75 to 80°F temperature, a high humidity, and reduced light. These, of course, represent the conditions peculiar to their original environment.

Calathea is sensitive to strong light; the *Maranta* is more tolerant in this respect.

76

They are propagated in spring by division of the clumps and of the rhizomes; reproduction by seed is utilized only by breeders.

They grow best in a mixture that is rich in organic matter and can be made of six parts organic matter and two parts top soil to one part sand. During the vegetative period they need frequent watering; this should be reduced from November to February, the period during which the plants are less active in growth.

Species and varieties. Among the best-known species, are:

C. angustifolia, native to tropical America, growing to 3 feet; *C. Bachemiana*, up to 9 inches, native to Brazil; *C. chantrieri*, also from Brazil,

has leaves grey and dark green and grows up to 12 inches; *C. luciana* from tropical America, grows up to 3 feet.

Calathea Mackoyana, coming from Brazil, is sometimes called the "peacock plant" because of the colours of the leaves.

C. ornata, native to Columbia, is vigorous and has large elliptical leaves.''

C. Veitchiana, from Peru, has large leaves with a purple colouration on the lower surface.

C. zebrina, with elegant stripes, does well in a temperate greenhouse.

They go well with *Maranta bicolor* and *M. leuconeura*, the Prayer Plant.

77

78

Palms

Kentia palms or howea

The *Kentias*, properly classified as a species of the genus *Howea*, even if the old name is still used, are the most important palms for indoor use and special decoration.

They are the pride of many greenhouses and botanical gardens where they are always admired, not least on account of their feathershaped, graceful leaves.

Origins. Once classified in the genus *Kentia*, they are now classified in the genus *Howea*: Palmaceae family.

They are native to Lord Howe Island in the Pacific, and include only two species, *H. Belmoreana* and *H. Forsteriana*.

Morphology. They are plants which grow large in their native habitat, having upright stems that may reach 35 feet or more. Characteristic is the presence of protruding roots and a thickening of the base.

They present terminal, large, numerous, pin-natifid, semi-pendulous leaves. The inflorescences are spadix shaped, 30 to 40 inches long, and are composed of flowers in groups of three. The fruit is a fibrous drupe.

Cultivation. *Kentias* are showy plants used in houses, churches, theatres and public buildings.

They are produced by seed that is rather slow to germinate and requires a loose and warm soil. The young plants are transplanted according to their growth, sometimes allocating two or more plants to a pot. Where the climate is frost free, they are cultivated in nursery beds and transplanted as needed to give them the space demanded for their development. They grow in organic matter mixed with a good top soil.

Once they have reached the commercial stage, they are potted for interior use. Instead of repotting adult plants, make additions of top soil. When they are kept in the greenhouse, they should be shaded and given frequent watering.

They dislike being disturbed at the roots so repotting often causes a setback. If additions of top soil cannot be made, as suggested above, then repotting must be carried out. A larger pot with new soil should be prepared—the bottom only being covered with soil at the outset of the operation. Then break the pot in which the palm is standing, and put the plant with its root ball undisturbed into the larger pot. Fill up with the remainder of the new soil.

Species and varieties. The two species of *Howea* are: *H. Belmoreana*, is of moderate size and reaches 10 feet in the greenhouse. It has large and greatly arched leaves as long as 6 feet, with numerous pointed leaf segments; and *H. Forsteriana*, which can reach 60 feet in height although from 6 to 15 feet is average. Its leaves are larger than the other species, with less numerous, but larger, leaf segments.

---

76. The delicate embroidery in the leaves of *Maranta leuconeura*, var. *Kerchoveana*.

77. Leaf of *Calathea insignis*.

78. *Calathea Mackoyana*, the "peacock plant".

79. Young specimen of the *Howea Forsteriana*.

80. Close up of *Howea Forsteriana*.

81. A pretty palm: the *Collinia elegans* (syn. *Chamaedorea elegans*) as undergrowth in a forest.

82. Palms of the species *Chamaerops humilis*.

79

80

81   82

83

84

Chamaerops, rhapsis and cocos

Chamaerops. Only one species exists, the *C. humilis*, otherwise known as the St. Peter Palm, the Fan Palm or the European Palm. It grows to between 10 and 30 feet, and can be treated as a greenhouse palm or as a half-hardy tree in sheltered, well-drained beds in the south of England. It can adjust itself to various environments, can endure exposure to bright sun and to cool temperatures. It is also tolerant of drought and is most suitable for decorating.

Rhapis. One of the fan-palms, so-called because of the shape of its leaves, it has a modest development and a matted appearance, is excellent for house decoration, where it can tolerate unfavourable conditions. Where frost-free climates prevail, it can be grown in the garden.

Cocos. A well-known plant is the species *C. nucifera*, the coconut, which is cultivated for its fruit and is familiar on account of the related

Arecastrum Romanzoffianum, particularly in the variety *Australe*, and *Syagrus Weddelliana*. These were previously classified as *Cocos* and are used in gardening; they are among the prettiest palms, with long, pinnate and very light leaves. They require warm temperature and fertile soil. The *Cocos* genus includes only the coconut, which is rarely grown indoors.

85

86

87

88

Chamaedoreas

This plant is native to Mexico and the countries of Central and South America.

Morphology. The genus *Chamaedorea* belongs to the Palmaceae. It includes about 70 species, of which about 10 are cultivated commercially.

They are small, erect, or procumbent palms, almost always bushy and often with a reed-like appearance. The leaves are mostly pinnatifid, sometimes simple. They are dioecious plants which means that the male and female flowers are on different plants. The fruit is a small, dry, or fleshy berry.

Cultivation. Like all palms, they can be easily reproduced by seed in the greenhouse. Use fresh seed that still maintains its germination ability, which is lost as the seed dries out. This is true for all the cultivated palms. Use a pot which has a cylindrical shape and is deep, for the tendency of the roots is to grow downward.

This plant prefers diffused light. The *Chamaedoreas* are not particularly demanding for water, but should be watered regularly.

For soil, use a mixture of five parts organic matter and two parts top soil to one part sand. Fertilize adult plants in the spring. The plant can be reproduced by seed sown 1 inch deep in pots.

Species and varieties. Among the most popular is the related *Collinia elegans* that is very familiar and very attractive; it is the smallest among the cultivated palms. It has dainty foliage and pinnate leaves that are as long as 11 inches.

Chamaedorea elatior is excellent for its tolerance to cold which allows it to live in the open ground in frost-free areas. Native to Mexico, it can grow to 30 feet.

89

90

83-84. *Phoenix canariensis* in a pot and in a grove along the Mediterranean coast.

85. The date palm: *Phoenix dactylifera.*

86. *Cocos nucifera* in its natural environment.

87. *Collinia elegans* (syn. *Chamaedorea elegans*).

89. Close up of the leaves of *Raphis.*

88, 90. The rigid, majestic elegance of the *Cycas revoluta* and a close up of the leaves in the same plant.

Phoenix

Phoenix dactylifera, the date palm, is the classical palm referred to in the Old and New Testaments and is symbolic of victory or triumph because of its use when Jesus triumphantly entered Jerusalem. It has always been well known as a fruit and is sometimes used as an ornamental plant.

Morphology. The genus *Phoenix* belongs to the *Palmaceae* family and includes about 12 species. They are mostly plants having tall stems, whose upper stem near the top is covered with the base of the stalks of the old leaves that have fallen. They have very large leaves that are pinnate, with whole, rigid segments that are obliquely attached to the rachis. The basal leaflets are often changed into thorns.

The very flashy inflorescences have an axillary spadix and each one of them is wrapped by a spathe until their development is completed.

They are deciduous plants. The fruit is a berry that is generally elongate.

Some *Phoenix* are of great value from an economic point of view.

Their tasty fruit, the date, is the main food of the Arab tribes of the desert. The milky liquid, sweet and fermentable, obtained from the stems, is transformed into an alcoholic drink.

Cultivation. Our concern here is for their ornamental value. They are cultivated with ease, starting with the seed that is placed to germinate in a pot in a humid and warm greenhouse.

Eventual pottings, using a soil formed from leaf mould, soil, and a little sand, will favour plant growth if care is taken to water abundantly.

Species and varieties. The best-known species is *Phoenix dactylifera*, the date palm, which is cultivated for its fruit. For decoration, it is surpassed by the widely used *P. canariensis*, native to the Canary Islands.

Also decorative are *P. aucaulis*, native to India, grows to 12 feet; *P. sylvestris*, also from India, that attains 40 feet; and *P. Roebelenii* that grows to 6 feet.

Cycas

Aesthetically similar to palms, even if botanically distant, and belonging to the Cycadaceae family, this genus has about 12 species, all native to lands with warm climates (China, East Indies, Australia, Japan, etc.). They are cultivated as ornamental plants throughout the world, either in the greenhouse or in the ground in those regions where the climate is mild. They need the same attention as palms.

The most famous species is the *Cycas revoluta*, having a developed trunk with a crown of very large leaves that are pinnate, leathery, and dark green.

Succulents and cacti

Succulents and cacti are plants which over many thousands of years have responded to unfavourable climatic conditions—hot sun, persistent drought, followed by torrential rain plus heat—by developing a form that conserves the moisture when the rainy season arrives. That moisture sustains the plant for the greater part of the yearly cycle.

Succulents have thick fleshy foliage and stems. Cacti—which are a type of succulent though not all succulents are cacti—can be distinguished by the fact that they have no leaves, apart from one genus, the Pereskia. This ensures that there is a minimum of transpiration. The thick epidermis and the small number of stomata also reduce loss of moisture. The stem of a cactus is ribbed, fluted or tubercular. It can expand or contract to accommodate the water coming up from the root system, and even in brief periods of torrential rain this tough accommodating stem does not split. In several species the roots, too, have become tuberous in the process of adaptation, and these act as moisture containers—sometimes being more voluminous than the stem of the plant.

Cacti are native to the Americas. They were introduced into Europe in the early seventeenth century and since then have spread to South Africa and Australia. Here in many places conditions are similar to those in the New World and this has resulted in the plants gaining a hold and proliferating. Today in some areas of Africa and Australia cacti have become such a nuisance that government-sponsored clearance schemes have been initiated.

Not all succulents grow on the earth's surface. Although the majority are found on sand or soil, a few rest on other plants, not as parasites but taking nutrients from the air.

Both cacti and succulents have adapted themselves well to greenhouse culture, and in recent years have established themselves as an extremely popular range of indoor plants. In Britain and in other countries in temperate zones they have to be given protection during the winter.

What is perhaps the most striking feature of cacti is that these leafless plants with curiously-shaped stems and forbidding thorns should produce such beautiful flowers. The flowers of the succulents are hardly ever seen.

Cacti are sub-divided into three types, the Pereskieae, *the* Opuniteae *and the* Cereeae, *and the last named has eight secondary divisions. Succulents are sub-divided into* Crassulaceae, Amaryllidaceae, Liliacceae, Portulacaceae, Aizoaceae-Mesembryanthemum, Asclepiadaceae, Aizoaceae, Euphorbiaceae *and* Compositae.

Sedum

Where there is a little soil, whether it be between two rocks that have been abandoned along a river or among the ruins of a crumbling building or on the narrow terrace of a steep Alpine wall, in the sun and with very little water, there we find *Sedums*.

Origins. This large genus, *Sedum*, (numbering 300 species, according to some, and 150 according to others), belongs to the *Crassulaceae* family.

It is a cosmopolitan, since it is present, although in varying degrees, on all continents. Many species are native to Europe, where they grow in difficult conditions.

Morphology. The *Sedums* are annual or perennial plants that are also herbaceous, but rarely suffruticose. They are fleshy, have erect or procumbent stems that can be simple or racemose and are sometimes quite matted to form a moss-like carpet.

The leaves have the most various shapes and have the ability to store water; they are fleshy, succulent, globous, cylindrical, with whole or toothed margins, and they are always stipulated.

Cultivation. In the past some species of *Sedum* have attracted interest as edible plants to be consumed fresh, and as constituents of popular medicines due to their emetic and antiscorbutic properties and their effectiveness as an external application for wounds. They are particularly appreciated in rock gardens, or as plantings in dry corners exposed to the sun, or on old walls or even for borders.

Their cultivation is extremely easy because *Sedums* have few demands. They are propagated easily by division of the clumps or by stem or root cutting. They grow on practically any substrate and they need little water.

The Alpine species and the ones of temperate climates can be cultivated in open ground all the year round. The tropical kinds need a winter shelter and can be cultivated in a greenhouse.

Species and varieties. About 30 species for garden or house are known. Among them are:

Sedum alpestre, native to the Alps, has white flowers and is suitable for Alpine gardens.

S. acre, sometimes called "pepper of the walls", is a species native to Morocco and now naturalized and widely found in gardens.

S. rupestre is native to the Alps; it has numerous yellow flowers.

S. Sieboldii, native to Japan, has a characteristic arrangement of the stems falling down like rays and flowers in late autumn.

S. caeruleum, is a very pretty and decorative little plant with small starry blue flowers.

S. anglieum has flowers white tinged with pink.

Other species are: *S. Telphium, S. Adolphii, S. praealtum,* and *S. album.*

---

91. *Sedum spurium* with blossoms.

92, 93. *Crassula arborescens* with the close view of the fleshy flowers.

94. Flower of *Crassula falcata.*

92   93

Crassulas

94

Crassula is a typical genus of the Crassulaceae family that includes numerous others cultivated for the decoration of gardens and houses.

Origins. *Crassulus* have been cultivated since they were introduced in Europe from South Africa. They came to Britain in the early eighteenth century.

Morphology. They are generally erect; the leaves are simple, opposed, sessile, cone-shaped, oval or triangular, fleshy, and glabrous or pubescent or scaly. The cymose or capitate inflorescences have small white or pinkish or yellow pentamerous flowers.

Cultivation. Their cultivation does not present difficulties. In warm regions they grow in the open, while in the north they must be placed in a temperate greenhouse during winter, or indoors.

They are generally propagated by cuttings in the sun, during the spring and summer months, or under glass at other times. Plant them in a soil formed from equal parts of fertile soil and clean sand, and water them sparingly during rooting.

The potting is done keeping in mind the necessity for good drainage and for a very light soil mixture without fertilizers, which may be made from three parts of sand and one part of peat to one part top soil.

Exposure to the sun is important since the plants are heliophylous, or sun-loving. This applies both to those that are cultivated in the open as well as to those cultivated in the green-house. Watering must be light because excessive and persistent humidity is ruinous. Abundant irrigations are useful during the growing period as long as they are not too frequent; always use water with a temperature similar to that of the surrounding air.

Particular care is given when repotting, if necessary in spring, and when pruning some species to make a bushy shape.

Species and varieties. The main species are:

Crassula arborescens, a plant with branches, a bare stem, and oval-elongate, dull glaucous or grey-greenish leaves and white flowers.

C. argentea, a plant which has a branched and brown stem, shiny green leaves that are oval-oblong with a short point, and flowers that bloom early (March, April).

C. falcata is a plant with a simple and non-branched stem, leaves that are sickle-shaped, opposed, and joined to the base in pairs, and abundant flowers that are red-crimson.

C. perfoliata is a plant with a simple stem, whose leaves are lanceolate, acuminate, and hollow on the upper part of the plant; the scented flowers are white.

C. lactea is a small, decorative shrub, with oval and light-green leaves; the flowers are in terminal clusters.

C. sarcocaulis is a small plant suited for rock gardens.

C. columnaris, with white flowers, grows up to 6 inches.

C. lycopodioides, greenish, grows up to 2 feet.

C. multicava, white flowers, grows up to 6 inches.

C. perforata, yellowish flowers, grows up to 4 feet.

C. pyramidalis, from 1 to 2 feet, has white flowers.

Another genus of the Crassulaceae family, *Rochea*, has similar requirements regarding cultivation and propagation to the *Crassulas*. The commercially grown species are:

R. coccinea, grows to 1 foot, and has scarlet flowers.

R. jasminea, from 6 to 9 inches, has white flowers.

R. versicolor, grows up to 2 feet, and has white and pink flowers.

Kalanchoes

This strange name, of Chinese derivation, refers to plants of more than 100 species that are spread not only in tropical areas, but also in South Africa, India and South America. They were first introduced into Britain at the end of the eighteenth century.

Morphology. The *Kalanchoes* are herbaceous, sturdy, and shrubby plants that have an erect stem. They have opposite, fleshy, sessile or petioled leaves.

The flowers are bright with very tiny corollas which are yellow, red-purplish or scarlet; they appear in inflorescences shaped like a paniculated umbrella, and are tetramerous. The fruit is a capsule with four carpels.

Cultivation. *Kalanchoes* are very pretty and interesting plants whose acceptance by the public is becoming greater and greater on account of the lasting quality of the plants in houses, and the long blooming period which can be obtained in the greenhouse nearly all the year round. The best position for the pots is close to the glass. Pots should be well-drained. A moderate temperature of 60 to 65°F between March and September is sufficient; whereas around 45 to 50°F is sufficient during the winter months.

The exposure should be to full sun, and the soil mixture should be the same as that given for the *Crassula* genus. Watering has to be abundant in the warm spring and summer months, must be progressively diminished after August, and then done sparingly in winter.

Since *Kalanchoes* tend to loose their leaves as they get older, pruning can be done after blooming, thus forcing the growth of new branches which will not, however, bloom as well.

For this reason, the practice is not at all widespread and it is better to use a stem cutting taken between June and August. In commercial greenhouses seed is sown in sandy soil, just covered with fine soil, in April.

Species and varieties. Of more than 100 species that have been catalogued, only about 12 have commercial value and these vary in colour of the flower.

Kalanchoe beharensis, native to Madagascar, is a plant widely cultivated on the Continent. It grows 25 to 30 inches tall and even more, with large, triangular leaves, and yellowish-green to white flowers.

K. flammea, native to Somalia, is about 15 inches tall and has yellow and orange-scarlet flowers. *K. thyrsiflora*, *K. laciniata*, *K. marmorata*, *K. lanceolata*, *K. pinnata* and *K. Blossfeldiana* are other very decorative species. *K. Schimperiana*, has white flowers and grows to 2 feet.

95

96

95. Young plants of *Kalanchoe pinnata*.

96. Close view of *Kalanchoe* with plantlets on the leaf margin.

97

98

99 100

Echeverias

Most species of this genus belong to the flora of Mexico and are named in honour of the Mexican botanist and painter, Attanasio Echeverria.

The genus *Echeveria* belongs to the *Crassulaceae* family and about 80 species are known, of which 20 are popular with gardeners. Some experts include them in the *Cotyledon* family.

Morphology. They are herbaceous plants which have a fleshy appearance, are almost always stemless, with fat and flattened leaves arranged in thick rosettes, green-greyish in colour.

The flowers are in loose racemes or in spikes or in paniculated umbels and have a pentamerous base. The corolla is angular with 5 corners, in yellow, orange or pink.

Cultivation. *Echeverias* are cultivated as house plants, but half-hardy species can be planted outside. They can be used successfully in rocky locations or in small groups as a border. If they are put close to stones, they are particularly suited for bedding. They are also suited for upright designs in sphagnum where they can be constructed as columns and used together with begonias and other coloured leaf plants.

They are cultivated all the year round in warmer areas, where the temperature never drops to freezing. In cool areas they must spend the winter under a shelter, in a greenhouse, or indoors. They are propagated by leaf cuttings or by separating the basal shoots.

Species and varieties. The most popular species are:

Echeveria glauca is caulous, with rosettes of $2\frac{1}{2}$ to 4 inches and leaves which are powdery greyish-green sometimes showing pinkish shades. The flowers are red and bloom in spring or autumn.

E. setosa is covered with white hairs from which its name is derived. The rosettes are almost globular; the red flowers bloom in July to August.

E. multicaulis has a hairy and greatly branched stem; the rosettes are large and loose with green leaves; the flowers are red with a winter blooming in warm places.

E. caespitosa (syn. *Cotyledon californica*) produces yellow flowers in the summer, and grows up to 1 foot.

E. farinosa has orange-red flowers, with silvery-white leaves, and is native to California.

E. gibbiflora has red flowers in the autumn and grows up to 2 feet.

E. elegans and *E. agavoides* are also species with ornamental value.

101

97. Flowers of *Kalanchoe Blossfeldiana*.

98. *Crassulaceae* are appreciated for the succulence of their leaves.

99. Flower beds bounded by *Echeverias*.

100. *Echeveria elegans* in cultivation.

101. The rosette shape of the *Echeveria*.

Aloe

This is a typical genus of the South African countryside that was first introduced in the sixteenth century. The long red and yellow tufts of its inflorescences and the characteristic acuminate leaves complement the sea in coastal regions of Africa and America.

Origins. The genus *Aloe* belongs to the Liliaceae family, which includes many plants of interest to gardeners. It numbers about 180 species native to Southern Africa, Madagascar, Arabia, India, Canary Islands and south western Mediterranean regions.

Morphology. Characteristic of the *Aloe* is the large variety of forms offered by their species. They are either stemless plants with more or less large basal leaves or they are tree-like plants with dichotomous branching. They have fleshy, thin leaves which are triangular in shape, more or less toothed, and sword-shaped or spiny on the margins and sometimes all over the surface. They are produced at the top of the stalk or arranged in a basal rosette.

Some grow to a considerable height with a fine display of tubular pendant flowers; others are small enough to be suitable for a dish garden.

The numerous flowers are in racemes or spikes on a long scape; they are brightly coloured in red or yellow and are often striped in paler shades. The fruit is a trivalved capsule containing numerous flattened and winged seeds.

The genus *Aloe* is of important medical and economic value. The *Aloes* not only have ornamental use, but are also in the official Pharmacopoeia as laxatives and eupeptics both in human and veterinary medicine. From the *Aloe* (*A. perfoliata*) come the fibres for bulky fabrics which have a local value, especially in India.

Cultivation. The *Aloe* species for gardens are of great interest because, to a greater or smaller degree, they are all ornamental. They are cultivated in full sun in warm climates and in greenhouses elsewhere.

Their shapes, plastic-like and with a morbid rigidity, go well even with modern architecture. Species of a smaller size are useful in the decoration of flats.

They are grown in a temperate greenhouse (42 to 50°F). They prefer a soil mixture that is sandy and well drained. The use of small, shallow pots, with a soil mix of leaf mould and top soil is suggested.

They should be moderately watered especially in winter; while in the greenhouse they require much light and a dry atmosphere. Transplanting is only done when plants become pot-bound.

Propagation takes place by division of the clumps, by offshoots or by cuttings. They can also be reproduced by seed at the end of winter in a hothouse.

Species and varieties. The most important ornamental species are briefly described: *Aloe africana*, native to South Africa, is tree-like and may reach 10 feet in height. It is popular in botanical gardens and blooms in summer.

A. ciliaris comes from South Africa. It is a tiny species very popular in the United States.

A. ferox is from South Africa; leaves are

104

grouped into thick rosettes having a glaucous colour; the thorns are reddish-brown and the flowers are orange.

A. humilis, of African origin, is a very pretty species in numerous varieties and hybrids. *A. humilis* var. *echinata* and *A. arborescens* var. *pachythyrsa* are worthy of mention for their large inflorescences.

A. variegata from South Africa is small and has lovely white markings. Other popular types include: *A. striata*, *A. vera* and *A. bravifolia*.

Haworthia

This genus bears the name of the English botanist A. H. Haworth, who was a great expert on cacti.

The plants are native to South Africa. *Haworthia* belongs to the Liliaceae family and includes about 60 species.

Morphology. These succulents are perennial, small-sized, stemless plants. The leaves are thick, fleshy, pointed or truncated; they are often covered with white and even transparent tubercles. They are arranged in the stipes in overlapped rows or arranged in basal rosettes.

The flowers are white, green, or striped with red, are arranged in simple or panicled racemes, and have a tubular shape. The fruit is a capsule containing compressed and angular seeds.

Cultivation. *Haworthias* are plants of ornamental interest and are particularly suited as house plants. They are attractive and very well-suited to room culture—given all the sun they can get. They also do well under artificial light. They need to be freely watered in summer, less so in winter.

Propagation is accomplished by vegetative means using root shoots or cuttings.

Reproduction by seeds is easy, but produces plants quite variable and unlike the parent plant.

Species and varieties. The most important species are:

Haworthia fasciata has rigid, leathery leaves that are sharp and have regular stripes given by white formations of tubercles.

H. margaritifera has very sharp leaves coloured with large white tubercles.

H. margaritifera var. *granata* has more crowded tubercles.

H. retusa has rather soft leaves which are rough on the back and truncate.

H. reinwardii has elongated rosettes and is a very attractive species.

H. viscosa has overlapping leaves in three rows.

102. Cactus greenhouse.

103. Inflorescence of the *Aloe*.

104. *Haworthia fasciata* with leaves, elegantly decorated by white tubercles.

105

106

107

108

Mesembryanthemum

Single daisies, Korean chrysanthemums, fig marigolds, or small gerberas. The nomenclature of *Mesembryanthemum* is very confusing.

Mesembryanthemum is a genus of the Aizoaceae family encompassing over 1,000 species.

Origins. They have a tropical origin and most of them come from South Africa. Some grow in rocky areas, others on sandy soils. Some are found near the sea. All are native to semi-arid tropics and subtropics.

Morphology. They are succulent, mostly herbaceous plants, sometimes tree-like and sometimes even without a stem, an extreme expression of a very advanced condition of xerophytism. They have fleshy, conical or pyramidial triangular leaves that are green or even glaucous, bluish or purple.

The flashy and very bright flowers are abundantly produced in different colours: white, yellow, and in all shades of red and pink to purple and orange. They have long and narrow petals that are very graceful and open up in the daylight only by the direct action of the sun.

The fruit is a capsule with a mechanical opening and closing of its valves in conditions of humidity. There is the exception of the *Carpobrotus edulis* and *C. acinaciformis* in which the fruit is fleshy and edible and is consumed by some African people; from this the plant receives its name "Hottentot Fig".

Some species have edible leaves, even though Mesembryanthemums are mainly used as ornamental plants for the garden as well as the house.

Cultivation. In sunny parts of the greenhouse or window of the house, using well-drained pots. Can be planted outdoors in sunny borders from June to September in sandy loam and leaf mould.

Propagation by seeds is done in April in a greenhouse where they are sown in sand while the humidity is increased. They are easily propagated by cuttings and by division.

Species and varieties. The most remarkable species of Mesembryanthemums are:

Carpobrotus acinaciformis, from South Africa but now naturalized in some warm countries; it produces beautiful pink-purple flowers.

Carpobrotus edulis, yellow or violet flowers and triangular leaves.

Cryophytum crystallinum, Ice Plant (so-called because of the presence on their light-green leaves of crystalline droplets), has bright chromatic effects; the flowers are white or pink.

Dorotheanthus Bellidiformis is a very beautiful species, appreciated for its abundant blooming with a palette of colours.

Lampranthus roseus is sometimes used to cover slopes with a compact carpet that is scattered with bright pink flowers.

Mesembryanthemum bifoliatum has rose-purple flowers, stems branching underground.

M. alboroseum, with white flowers, has a shrubby habit and grows to 5 inches.

M. paardebergebse, with rose-coloured flowers in dense cymes, grows to 8 inches.

M. Putterillii has ascending or decumbent branches, produces rose-purple solitary flowers and grows to 9 inches.

M. verruculatum has branches either crooked or twisted, and produces bright yellow flowers.

Opuntias

This genus is native to the American continent from Canada to the Straits of Magellan. Over 250 species are described. They are known by the common names Prickly Pear, Tuna or Cholla.

Morphology. The genus *Opuntia* belongs to the family of the Cactaceae and has plants of variable sizes and shapes which display erect to prostrate habits and range from small to tall, even reaching the appearance of shrubs up to 15 to 20 feet. They have fibrous or thickened roots. The stems and the branches are formed by many smaller ones so that they look like large and fleshy leaves attached to one another. The actual leaves, instead, are small and drop early. On the sides of the stem numerous thorns are borne that can be solitary or in groups, bare or characteristically covered and accompanied by fuzzy bristles. Some species are thornless.

The flowers grow on the distal parts of the areoles, and have green sepals or a colour which is very close to that of the petals, usually a flashy green, yellow or red. The fruit is a fleshy globous berry that can be ellipsoidal or ovoidal, spiny or spineless, with many seeds buried in the pulp.

Cultivation. Some hardy species of *Opuntia* are cultivated in warm areas in sunny, well-drained rockeries from March onwards. Others are cultivated for decorative purposes in the sunny part of the greenhouse. They need well-drained soil that is slightly alkaline.

They can very easily be propagated because, from every section that is detached from the stem, one can obtain a new plant. Waterings should not be too frequent or too abundant; they need much light and full sun.

Species and varieties. Among the most interesting greenhouse species are: *Opuntia vulgaris*, native to South America, has a modest size, with yellow flowers and edible fruit. It is used as understock for grafting or more delicate species.

O. cylindrica comes from Ecuador and Peru. It is a very decorative plant on account of its stem that has cylindrical sections and its scarlet flower. It is used as understock for grafting.

O. Ficus indica is the famous Indian fig found in all warm regions.

O. diademata presents odd pimples on the leaf sections.

O. Tuna, *O. leucotricha*, and *O. Whipplei* are other ornamental species.

105-108. Palette of colours in the flowers of *Mesembrayanthemum* and related genera.

109. *Opuntia tunicata*, showing strong spines.

110. *Opuntia Bigelowii.*

111-114. Close-up of fruits and flowers of *Opuntia* species.

109

110

111

110

112

113

114

115

116

117

Cereus

Plants with stylized forms that suggest modern architecture, *Cereus* are a distinctive feature of the countryside of Central and South America and of the islands of the West Indies. In Britain they are greenhouse plants.

The genus *Cereus* belongs to the *Cactaceae* family and includes about 30 species, some of an interesting ornamental appearance.

Many plants are called "Cereus" while they really belong to related genera such as *Echinocereus*, *Selenicereus* and *Echinopsis*.

Morphology. Perennial, succulent plants that have a slender appearance (some of them look like gigantic candelabra). The stalks are furrowed by ribs whose number varies from 4 to 9; they can be more or less branched and are always without leaves.

The large showy flowers appear along the ribs and have a tubular receptacle that can be green or dark lead-green, glabrous or hairy; the numerous petals are in bright colours. Each blossom lasts only one night. The fruit is a fleshy berry that contains numerous small black seeds.

Cultivation. *Cereus* were first cultivated in Britain in the late seventeenth century. They need well-drained pots and a sunny position in the greenhouse or window, and should be transferred to larger pots every two or three years.

Their culture follows the direction already given for the other cacti. They need a soil that has little organic matter and is always well drained so that injury from excess water is avoided.

Propagation is by seeds or by cuttings. *Cereus* are excellent understocks in grafting more delicate *Cactaceae*.

Species and varieties. The most popular species are: *Cereus peruvianus*, which is seen in botanical gardens and grows up to 40 feet.

C. azureus grows to 3 or 4 feet, has a thin stem that is branched from the base, and has a bluish-green colour when it is young and a dark green colour when it becomes older.

C. kewensis has pink and white flowers, a hybrid.

C. variabilis has green and red flowers.

C. alacriportanus has white flowers, tinged red, grows up to 6 feet and has a five-ribbed, slightly wavy stem.

C. coerulescans grows to 5 feet, and has day-flowering flowers, reddish on outside, white inside.

---

115. Greenhouse of cactus plants with *Echinocactus* and *Cereus*.

116. *Cereus peruvianus* var. *monstruosus*.

117. *Cactaceae* remind us of thorns and an arid climate.

118. The attractive bloom of the *Cactaceae* is a reward for the short duration of the flowers.

119. *Cephalocereus senilis*.

120. *Cephalocereus senilis* in company with other cacti.

119

118

120

Cephalocereus (Old man cactus)

This genus includes species whose stem is covered by little areoles with spines mixed with long whiskers, and with a terminal tuft that is larger and makes the adult plants look like the hair on an old man's head. It is one of the most attractive of the cacti and lends itself to miniature gardens and terrariums.

Origins. The *Cephalocereus* genus belongs to the Cactaceae family and includes about 20 species that are native to Mexico, Ecuador and Brazil.

Morphology. They are plants with a columnar stem that can be simple or branched, ribbed or spreading, and with long bristles.
The flowers are numerous and variously coloured according to the species. The fruits are globular, small berries.

Cultivation. Culture is not difficult and is the same as for other Cactaceae; the only proviso concerns temperature which must always be above 50°F.

Species and varieties. The most commonly cultivated species are: *Cephalocereus senilis*, which is better known by the name of "Old Man Cactus"; and *C. languinosus*, *C. Royenii* and *C. Russelianus*.

Mammillarias

These are outstanding plants because of the perfect symmetry of their shape, and this makes them fine house plants.

Origins. Most species are native to Mexico and Central America.

The *Mammillaria* genus belongs to the Cactaceae family and numbers 200 species.

Morphology. *Mammillarias* are small sized plants having a spherical or cylindrical shape. The stems bear many protuberances that look like tubercles or mammilla and are arranged in spirals which present at the top a small tomentose areole that bears thorns set as a halo of rays. The thorns are interesting for their varied shape and for their range in colour from black to white and from yellow to red.

The flowers are white, red or yellow; they are small and are shaped like short bells arranged like a crown that is usually turned toward the top of the branch.

The fruits are small berries that are red, white or rose; they are very attractive and often a crown of fruits accompanies a crown of flowers emphasizing the ornamental value of the plant.

Cultivation. These plants are not difficult to grow; they are much in demand as a decoration both in the exotic rock garden, where they show their beauty, and in the house. They are propagated by basal offshoots that grow as a new plant.

One must remember that the *Mammillarias*

develop well in large shallow pots and are particularly appreciated if they are in a large colony.

They do not have particular needs as far as soil is concerned, although almost all species like the presence of lime.

A suitable mixture can be formed by garden mould, well-decomposed leaf mould and sand in equal amounts with the addition of lime. Good drainage, little water, and much sun will ensure success.

Species and varieties. Among the best-known species are:

Mammillaria spinosissima, of Mexican origin, has a cylindrical shape, lead-coloured leaves and red flowers.

M. microcarpa, native to Texas and Arizona, is globose or cylindrical and branched at the base with purplish-red flowers.

M. prolifera (= *M. pusilla*) is very common and is appreciated for its high decorative value. It has a spheroidal or ovoid shape and is matted with reddish or yellowish thorns and yellow flowers.

---

121. Specimen of *Mammillaria fragilis* that looks like a mysterious "totem pole".

122. Here is an example of how the peculiar artistry of Nature covers up the big leafless stems of the Cactaceae with geometrically arranged thorns.

123-124. *Mammillaria triangularis* and detail of areoles bearing thorns.

125

126

127

Echinocactus

These are the cacti that attract the most attention from visitors to exotic gardens, because of their shape and large dimensions.

Origins. The plants of this genus belong to the Cactaceae family and are native to southwest U.S.A. and Mexico.

Morphology. The plants are globose or cylindrical; they are leafless, depressed at the apex, with very evident mostly vertical ribs that are covered with strong straight thorns.

The flowers are arranged at the top; they are small or large, mostly yellow or shades of yellow; they open up in full sun and persist longer than those of other Cactaceae.

Cultivation. Interest in these plants is exclusively for their ornamental value. Propagation takes place by seeds, because the *Echinocactus* do not produce basal shoots, or by cuttings of stems inserted in small pots of sandy soil kept almost moist in summer.

They are very demanding as far as heat is concerned, but they enjoy semi-sunny locations. They need abundant watering during the summer, especially in the warmer hours of the day.

A suitable substratum is formed by mixing two parts of coarse sand and one part of peatmoss with one part wood duff and one part loam.

Species and varieties. *Echinocactus Grusonii*, has a globous shape and large dimensions; its thorns are grouped in fours, are somewhat trans-

parent, and sulphur yellow; the flowers are yellow and red.

E. horizonthalonius, with modest dimensions, is globose or short-cylindrical when mature, with brown or reddish thorns.

E. ingens, grows to 5 feet high and 4 feet in diameter, with brown spines and yellow flowers.

---

125. *Echinocactus Grusonii* and *Euphorbia*.

126-127. Symmetrical structure of *Echinocactus* with flowers arranged on top.

128-130. Close-up of *Echinocactus* in bloom.

128

129

130

131

133

Epiphyllum

This is a group of cacti that both in appearance and in cultural requirements departs from the groups previously described. Furthermore they have a familiar appearance because they are commonly cultivated along with related genera, such as *Zygocactus*, *Schlumbergera*, etc.

Origins. They are epiphtic plants and live in tropical forests of Central America. They belong to the Cactaceae family and they are succulent, bushy plants which have flattened branches with stalks that look like long crenate or toothed leaves.

Their very pretty flowers are large, white, red, pink or yellow, very numerous and arranged around the margins of the stems. The fruits, of an elongated shape, are red and contain many black seeds.

Cultivation. Cultivation is not difficult. The plants need sunny locations and moderate waterings during the summer. They can live outdoors or in a cold frame in summer, but in September they need to be taken indoors where only the minimum amount of water should be applied.

Contrary to other cacti, they need a soil rich in organic matter which can be a mixture of peat, rotted manure, leaf mould, and loam in equal amounts with the addition of a little sand. Propagation can be by seed or by cuttings.

A curiosity is the grafting on to *Pereskia aculeata*, to form little trees having a considerable ornamental effect.

Species and varieties. Among the most important species are: *Epiphyllum Ackermannii*, with white and crimson flowers, and *E. oxypetalum* with pink and white, scented petals. There are numerous attractive hybrids.

E. anguliger has yellow, fragrant flowers; *E. Hookeri*, native to Brazil, has white fragrant flowers.

E. stenopetalum has flowers that are 1 foot long, with a tube 8 inches in length, white within and greenish outside.

E. pittieri has hyacinth-scented blooms up to 7 inches long and 6 inches across, star-shaped, green and white in colour. The branches are notched and toothed.

134

E. crenatum grows to 3 feet and is of erect habit with shallowly-toothed stems. The fragrant flowers, creamy-white inside and greenish outside, are up to 4 inches across. It does well out of doors between June and September.

131. One of the cacti group that is widely grown: *Schlumbergera*, related to *Epiphyllum*.

132. Flower of *Epiphyllum*.

133. Spathe and inflorescence of *Anthurium Scherzerianum*.

134-137. Spathes and inflorescences of *Anthurium Andreanum*.

138. Cultivation of *Anthurium* in the greenhouse.

Flowering plants

Anthurium

The name is taken from the Greek, meaning tail flower, this being based on the tail-like spadix of the genus. There are some 500 species in the genus, but since the vast majority demand an extremely hot and moist atmosphere they have not been cultivated as houseplants, apart from those listed below. Beautiful foliage is a mark of some of the plants; others are climbers.

Originating in the tropical and subtropical regions of Central America, the genus belongs to the Araceae family, and has numerous species which are perennials, with erect or climbing stems. The leaves are entire, lobate or divided and have an oval, cordate, arrow-like or spear-like shape; they are green or in metallic shades and almost aways have long stalks.

The inflorescence is an upright, wrapped or wrinkled spadix with a large, green, yellow, red or purple spathe. The fruit is a berry.

They were introduced into Britain in the nineteenth century and since that time have grown in popularity.

Cultivation. Demanding constant attention, they are plants for warm, humid greenhouses at day temperatures of from 70 to 75°F and from 65 to 70°F at night. They require diffused light for which it is necessary to shade the greenhouse. The creeping species need supports such as a stake lined with sphagnum or osmunda fibre.

Anthuriums are grown in a light, porous mixture that is formed of chopped sphagnum, tiny pieces of osmunda roots, top soil in equal amounts, plus sand. Some experts advise the addition of charcoal in the case of *Anthuriums* for flowers, or the composition of a rather clayey soil for the foliage varieties. It is essential to drain the pot carefully and place the plants so that the crown will be slightly below the top edge of the pot, filling up the space that remains with sphagnum. This favours the development of advantitious roots that develop in the axil of the leaves after the plants bloom.

Abundant watering during the vegetative period and frequent liquid fertilization is given. The annual repotting is dependent on the growth and vigour of the plant.

Anthuriums propagate by seeds that are sown shortly after picking; otherwise they lose their viability. Seeding is done in late summer or autumn in well-drained containers filled with leaf mould and sphagnum with charcoal and sand added, at a temperature of 80°F.

They are also propagated by cuttings in June to July, using all the stem, including the part underground; layering can also be used or the clumps can be divided.

Species and varieties. Certain kinds are grown for flowers and others for leaves. Among the *Anthuriums* for flowers are *A. Andreanum*, which also has a pretty foliage, and *A. Scherzerianum*

(Flamingo flower); both have numerous hybrids. *A. Scherzerianum* is sometimes called "Painter's Palette" because of the beauty of its wax-like flowers.

Among the foliage *Anthuriums* are *A. crystallinum*, with very large leaves that are velvety green with light veins, and *A. Veitchii*, with huge, metallic green leaves that are darker when the plant is mature.

Among creeping species are *A. miquelianum* and *A. Kalbreyeri*.

135

136

Callas

After many taxonomic changes, the genus *Calla* has been given the name of *Zantedeschia* in honour of the Italian botanist Francesco Zantedeschi; the old name Calla has become the common name.

The Calla or Arum Lily whose inflorescence looks like an extraordinary shell, has a proud appearance whenever it is seen alone, but, once it is put close to other exotic plants, especially outdoors along water streams or around the edges of ponds, it acquires a warm flashy splendour that recalls its African origin.

Origins. The *Zantedeschia* genus belongs to the Araceae family. Membership includes 8 species which are native to Southern Africa and have been cultivated for ornamental purposes for several centuries.

Morphology. They are perennial ornamental plants that are typical of humid, swampy areas; they have a large rhizome from which the leaves arise on a long, spongy stalk.

The leaf is large, arrowhead-shaped, lanceolate, or heart shaped with a wavy border; its colour is a uniform green or spotted with white or yellow.

The spadix inflorescence includes a white, yellow, or rose spathe, A-shaped and rounded at the base, terminating in a point that is curved downwards; the inflorescence is carried by an erect peduncle that is as long as, or a little longer than, the leaves. The fruit is a berry.

Cultivation. Callas are cultivated as pot-plants or in open ground during the warm weather, or as cut flowers.

Propagation is by seeds, sown immediately after maturation, but more often propagation is by division of the rhizomes. The rhizomes themselves are planted in large pots filled with a mixture rich in humus. A recommended compost has equal parts loam, cow manure and silver sand.

It is a greedy plant and when flowering should be given plenty of water and liquid manure.

It is important to provide these plants with a period of rest after blooming which can be initiated by diminishing the frequency of waterings.

Planted outdoors in May, the calla flowers from June to September and is brought indoors in October.

After blooming, the plant is allowed to become

139

dry. The rhizomes are then taken out of the ground and placed in pots that are full of sand to prevent them from drying out. They are replanted in the spring.

If a stimulant is called for—and some experts recommend a weekly stimulant when flowering —a choice can be made from 1 teaspoonful of a recommended fertilizer (such as Clay's), half-anounce of Peruvian guana, or one-quarter ounce of sulphate of ammonia or nitrate of soda to 1 gallon of water.

Species and varieties. The best-known calla is the *Zantedeschia aethiopica* of which there are several varieties: *minor*, 12 to 15 inches tall; *devoniensis*, that is scented; *candidissima*; *grandiflora*; and *gigantea*, with a beautiful effect be-

cause of the shape and colour of the spathe.

Z. albo-maculata has acuminate and whitespotted leaves.

Z. melanoleuca has oval lanceolate leaves that are spotted with white and a spathe with a purple spot at the base.

Worthy of mention are the *Z. Elliottiana*, with a yellow spathe, and *Z. Rehmanni*, with a rosy-purple spathe. *Elliottiana*, native to South Africa, is the taller of the two, growing to 3 feet.

---

139. A magnificent plant of blooming *Calla*.

140. Young sprout of *Zantedeschia Elliottiana*.

141, 142. *Calla*: a close-up of the spathe.

140

141

142

Euphorbias

This is a very large group of plants all native of tropical, subtropical and temperate regions of the world, where many of them have been known since antiquity because of their medicinal properties.

All the *Euphorbias* secrete a whitish caustic latex that is in some species extremely poisonous. Some hardy species are weeds in gardens, lawns, and pastures. About 100 are considered ornamental.

Morphology. Belonging to the Euphorbiaceae family, the *Euphorbia* genus is variable, including herbaceous annuals, perennials, shrubby and tree-like arboreal plants, and large-leaved and Cactus-like plants.

Characteristic of the plants is the cup-shaped inflorescence that is formed by a peduncled female flower surrounded by many male mono-stamened flowers; this is emphasized by leaf bracts which are more or less developed and greenish or brightly coloured.

Cultivation. The species of the *Euphorbia* genus that are of concern here are those cultivated for cutting flowers or for pot plants.

Undoubtedly *E. pulcherrima*, commonly called *poinsettia*, the popular Christmas flower which, together with *E. fulgens* and *E. splendens*, are the most famous and most cultivated.

Because of their various forms, *Euphorbias* have different demands and consequently different techniques of cultivation from species to species. Propagation of greenhouse species is by cuttings. It is advisable to immerse the cuttings in water for a few hours to eliminate the coagulated latex from the cut. The soil must be a good top soil, with the addition of organic matter. In the vegetative period, frequent watering and liquid fertilizations are required. *Euphorbia fulgens* has similar requirements whereas *E. splendens* is grown as described for succulents. Hardy species are propagated in a cold frame.

Species and varieties. *Euphorbia pulcherrima* (Poinsettia) is a magnificent shrubby plant that attracts our attention by the bright colour of its large red-scarlet bracts.

E. fulgens is cultivated because of its numerous flowers that are carried by elegant racemes.

E. splendens is very common and noted for its spiny stems.

Other interesting *Euphorbias* are the *E. abyssinica*, the *E. resinifera*, the *E. tridentata* that have the requirements of the Cactaceae.

Hardy species for sunny rockeries and dry banks include *E. Cyparissias*, yellow flowers, height 2 feet; *E. Myrsinites*, yellow flowers, of trailing habit; and *E. Wulfenii* that grows to 3 feet and bears yellow flowers.

143. *Euphorbia splendens.*

144. Spiny branches and inflorescence of *Euphorbia splendens.*

145. The classical and widely-spread inflorescence of the *Euphorbia pulcherrima*, the very popular Christmas flower.

146. *Euphorbia resinifera.*

147

Saintpaulia

Like the last born in a large family who attracts all the attention, so the *Saintpaulia*, that arrived from the Kilimanjaro mountains around the end of last century, has been greeted with admiration by gardeners and seedsmen. The credit for the discovery of this plant in 1892 goes to Baron von Saint Paul-Illaire.

Morphology. Known as the African violet, the *Saintpaulia* genus belongs to the Gesneriaceae family and has 20 species, of which the most typical is *S. ionantha.*

The plants are small, perennial, and herbaceous; they grow to about 6 inches in height. They have leaves that are oval, with a fleshy petiole, dark green, hairy, and arranged in a rosette.

The flowers, on a cymose inflorescence, have a monopetalous corolla that is irregular, has 5 lobes, and is large campanulate. The colour of the flowers ranges from white and pink to purple with bright yellow stamens. The fruit is an oblong capsule with small ellipsoidal seeds.

Cultivation. The interest in this pretty little plant is justified by the dainty beauty of its leaves and flowers, by its long period in bloom and by its tolerance of indoor conditions.

The *Saintpaulia* reproduces well by leaf cuttings taken at any season of the year. They are placed in peat and sand at a temperature of 75 to 80°F. Eventually they are potted in a light mixture of leaf mould, peat, soil and sand. Blooming takes place for most of the year, but particularly throughout the summer.

During its vegetative period it has to be watered normally, being careful not to wet the leaves that are very delicate. The plants are grown at 70 to 75°F in diffused light. During the rest period, they should be kept at 55 to 60°F and little water given.

Species and varieties. The best-known species of this genus is *S. ionantha,* already mentioned, of which varieties with white as well as pink and violet flowers are known. The flowers can be simple or double flowers, and the leaves are variegated. Its most popular varieties are *albescens* (white flowers), *purpurea* (purple flowers), and *violescens* (deep violet flowers). *S. pusilla* is a beautiful bluish-violet species.

148

149

150

151

Hoya

This plant attracts attention because of its almost artificial-looking flowers and attractive foliage.

Origins. The *Hoya* genus belongs to the Asclepiadaceae family and has about 70 species, all native to the Far East. A few of them are cultivated in greenhouses or as a house plant. They were introduced into Britain in the nineteenth century.

Morphology. *Hoyas* are plants having usually a climbing or creeping habit, with persistent leaves that are oval-shaped and of a leathery consistency.

The single, small, starred flowers with a brightly coloured centre are arranged in compact axillary, umbrella-shaped inflorescences; characteristic is the waxy appearance of the corollas and their delicate fragrance. The fruits are follicles containing seeds with a pappus.

Cultivation. Interesting, even if little-grown at present, they are cultivated for the beauty of the flowers and are very successful as house plants.

147-150. The African violet, botanically known by the name of *Saintpaulia ionantha*, has varieties with violet, pink and white flowers, either single or double.

151-152. *Hoya carnosa* is an exotic looking plant whose flowers have a wax-like appearance.

If taken care of, they last well.

They are propagated by cuttings, or by layering their long stems. They grow best in a light textured soil that is rich in organic matter, made of three parts organic matter, one part top soil, and one-half part sand. The soil must be well drained. They grow best in light shade; blossoming occurs in summer. Usually grown in pots, they can be trained on a trellis. Indeed, some experts recommend that they are grown only as climbers and if this is done a strong trellis is needed for the mature plant is heavy. If the greenhouse atmosphere is dry there is a danger the plant will be attacked by mealybugs. Badly infested leaves must be burned; those not so badly attacked can be treated successfully by wiping with cottonwool, soaked in methylated spirit, fixed on to a cocktail stick.

For gardeners who are installing fluorescent light systems, the *Hoya* genus has proved almost indispensable. They respond well to the artificial light, perhaps too well, as they are apt to grow out of the field of light.

This is a plant that responds to frequent syringing or having its leaves washed with milk diluted with water. As soon as buds appear the strength of the plant should be maintained by frequent applications of a liquid fertiliser until the flowering season is ended.

Once every three or four years the older plants should be repotted if they show signs of being out of condition. In any case a top-dressing of fertilizer should be given.

152

Species and varieties. Among the best-known species is *Hoya carnosa* (wax flower or honey plant), undoubtedly the most popular species for its "wax flowers" that are white with a rose centre and are very delicately scented. Varieties include *variegata* and *exotica*, and cultivar "Silver Pink". They are suitable for hanging baskets.

H. imperialis, with large, brown-purple flowers having a creamy white crown, is more demanding than *Hoya carnosa* because it requires a warmer temperature.

H. bella is a bushy, more dwarf species. Other species are *H. globulosa*, *H. multiflora* and *H. bandaensis*.

H. australis (otherwise known as *H. Dalrympliana*) white flowers tinged with pink, is native to Australia.

153

154

155

156

157

158

Pelargonium

These plants have red, pink, white and multi-coloured flowers. They are easily grown in boxes on a balcony, either individually or as a mass planting in a garden, in a pot on the window sill, or in an ornamental jar on the patio. They can be grown in any sunny location and will flower reliably.

Geranium is the common name, but botanically they belong to the genus *Pelargonium*, of the Geraniaceae family (the *Geranium* genus includes native and cultivated species that have minor importance as garden plants).

The scientific name *Pelargonium* derives from the Greek and means "stork", in the same way that Geranium means "crane" because of the likeness of the seeds of these plants to the long beaks of these long-legged birds.

Origins. It is a very large genus with many natural species, but today we grow hybrids and improved cultivars; there are many available and the number is increasing through hybridization.

The first species of *Pelargonium* introduced in Europe came from the Colony of the Cape, and was probably the *P. zonale*.

Morphology. *Pelargoniums* are perennial, shrubby plants, with herbaceous or woody, erect or procumbent stems. Their leaves have different shapes according to the species or to the varieties; they can be opposed or alternate, simple or compound, lobate or entire or indented.

The flowers are irregular and are axillary, peduncled, and in umbels; the calyx has 5 sepals, the corolla has 5 petals with all the shades of the red, from pink to dark violet; in addition, white and sometimes yellow appear in them. The very long fruit is pentacarpellary and dehiscent.

Cultivation. The cultivation of the geranium is not difficult even if its great popularity is more a demonstration of tolerance than of care. Its propagation is by seeds or by cuttings. Reproduction by seed is mainly used in the development of new cultivars.

The cuttings can be taken in spring or autumn, but the optimum time varies with the location and method of growing. Once the cuttings have rooted, they are placed in pots and, in the case of large flowered geraniums, they are topped—leaving three buds to grow into branches.

Species and varieties. *Pelargonium zonale* is the most common geranium; it has a busy appearance and an erect growth habit. In favourable conditions it can form shrubs that can even reach 6 feet in height.

The typical species is very rare, since the culture is today dominated by many cultivars that are derived from crossing the *P. zonale* with the *P. inquinans*.

We can separate the geraniums according to the colours of the leaves into varieties with silver, three-coloured, lead-coloured leaves, etc. The zonal pelargoniums can also be distinguished in their dwarf varieties.

P. peltatum is the classical ivy geranium that is suitable for decorating porches, terraces, walls and is used in hanging baskets. Its varieties are numerous.

P. domesticum is known by its common name of Martha Washington Geranium. This is a very pretty plant and is cultivated today in many varieties; it flowers only once a year.

Numerous geraniums have scented leaves and the range of their scents is great. They belong to many species among which are *P. odoratissimum*, with white flowers, height 1½ feet; *P. crispum* sometimes called Lemon-Scented, with rose-coloured flowers, height up to 3 feet; *P. graveolens*, flowers rose and purple, height from 2 to 3 feet; *P. Radula*, called Balsam-scented, flowers and height similar to *graveolens*; *P. capitatum*, flowers rose and purple, foliage rose-scented; and a hybrid, *P. citriodorum*, with white flowers and citron-scented foliage.

---

153. The classical and traditional geranium is the *Pelargonium zonale*.

154. Cutting of *Pelargonium zonale*.

155. Cutting of ivy-leaved geranium (*Pelargonium peltatum*).

156. The delicate flower of the Martha Washington Geranium, botanically *Pelargonium domesticum* (syn. *P. grandiflorum*).

157, 158. Two cultivars of *Pelargonium*.

Rhododendrons and Azaleas

Here there is a conflict in terminology. Many people call them Azaleas but botanically they are named Rhododendrons.

Origins. The genus *Rhododendron* belongs to the Ericaceae family and has so many species that disagreement exists concerning their number. It is native to a wide area including China, Korea, Japan, India and other Asiatic zones, and to several parts of Europe and North America.

Morphology. Rhododendrons are shrubs or small trees. They have alternate leaves that often are close together at the top of the branches; they are entire, leathery, deciduous or persistent.

Their large and flashy flowers have many colours: white, pink, red, violet, yellow; they can be solitary or more often grouped into corymbs. The calyx has five sepals and an irregular corolla that is funnel-shaped, tubular, bell-shaped, sub-rounded. The fruit is an oblong capsule.

Cultivation. Azaleas are a very popular ornamental species either for the garden or for cultivation in the greenhouse. This book is confined to the cultivation of house plants only and not of plants for all uses. We shall therefore briefly deal with the forcing of types suitable as potted plants.

The varieties available are botanically very heterogeneous and result from much hybridization. They are grouped into sections according to certain morphological characteristics. *Rhodo-*

dendron indicum, *R. Kaempferi*, *R. molle*, *R. Simsii* and *R. obtusum* are all species used in developing our present day types. *R. indicum*, native to Japan and with flowers red to scarlet, grows to 6 feet; *R. Simsii*, known as the Indian Azalea has rose-red flowers and grows to 5 feet; and *R. obtusum*, native to Japan, height up to 3 feet, flowers varying from purple through reds and pink to white.

There are numerous small species suitable for the rock garden, all evergreen. Recommended are *R. calostrotum* with bright purple flowers; and *R. chryseum* with bright yellow flowers.

Azaleas require an acid soil with a pH of 4.0 to 5.0. Peat is excellent to use. Perfect drainage is required.

Cuttings are taken in July and August from outdoor plants, or in the spring after flowering of the plants that were grown in the greenhouse.

They may require two to three years to become large-sized flowering plants.

In their second year they can be placed outdoors and periodically pruned to become an attractive plant. During all the period of cultivation, azaleas demand a great deal of water.

Forcing is done from Christmas to Easter, after allowing a dormant period of from at least six to eight weeks.

159-163. The azaleas, botanically *Rhododendrons*, with their beautiful flashy flowers of different colours and long duration.

Orchids

The Orchidaceae *family has more than 500 genera and includes more than 20,000 species.*

The name derives from one of the genera: Orchis. *According to mythology, Orchis was a young man who tried to approach a priestess of Bacchus; he was discovered and the god had him killed by wild animals, and later transformed him into an orchid flower.*

The family of Orchidaceae *is widely spread all over the world, with terrestrial plants in temperate and cold climates and epiphytic plants in tropical climates.*

In the second half of the nineteenth century, a new era for the cultivation of orchids began with the production of the first interspecific and intergeneric hybrids. Today the cultivation of orchids continues to meet a keen demand and generates the same degree of enthusiasm that was characteristic of the pioneers. The great value of these plants is the very pretty and bizarre shape of the flower, the enchanting colour and their long-lasting quality.

Because of the large number of genera, their very different shapes and the varied environment in which they live, it is impossible to give a description for every species. We give a few comments concerning the vegetative organs and the flowers.

Roots. *We distinguish normal roots from aerial. The normal roots are similar to those of other plants, but they are characterized by the presence of a mycorrhiza symbiosis that is present with the first stages of development of the seed and without which, in nature, the young plants cannot take root.*

The aerial roots are useful for absorbing water, both as a liquid and from humid air; if they have chlorophyll they take on an assimilatory function and sometimes also a support function.

Root tubercles. *There is another transformation of the roots frequently found in Orchidaceae and is the result of the apparent growing together of numerous, simple roots. Their function is to store reserve substances.*

Stems, rhizomes, pseudobulbs. *Orchid stems can be monopodial (the main axis develops more than the lateral ones) or sympodial (the lateral axis overtakes the main one).*

Other special formations are the pseudobulbs, organs with different shape and dimensions, but more commonly ovoidal. They are tuberized stems

and have a reserve function. Solitary or grouped, the leaves are present at the time of the pseudobulb in various numbers depending on the species.

Leaves. *Leaves vary in shape, width and colour and are generally sessile, single, and persistent. In many species the leaf appears glaucous, marbled, dotted and variegated.*

Flowers, inflorescence. *Bizarre and stupendous, they have the strangest shapes, but nevertheless they always look original and very elegant, even though they sometimes appear monstrous and cold. Their structure is complicated and is the result of transformations in function to allow insect pollination. With a few of the larger types, pollination is by birds.*

*The flowers can be solitary (*Cypripedium) *or in axillary, terminal or basal inflorescences. The male organs grow together with the female and are often transformed into petaloid organs called staminodes.*

The most developed petal is called the lip or labellum and takes on different shapes. The ovary is inferior, tricarpellary and is twisted into a spiral.

The cultivation of orchids is not easy. It is necessary for each species to be grown under conditions simulating their native environment as far as the growing medium and the climate (temperature, humidity, light, ventilation) are concerned, although they are tolerant plants. The technique differs whether one wants to cultivate terrestrial or epiphytic orchids.

Greenhouse temperatures may be hot, temperate, or cold; growing substratum may be sphagnum osmunda fibre, decayed oak or beech leaves, and peat, or a mixture of these.

Reproduction of seeds, once the symbiotic function of the mycorrhizia endotrophic fungus, is not facilitated by nutrient cultures of agaragar or gelatine, and is strictly for experts.

A tuberoid body, called a protocorm, develops from the seed in about two months, from which, in 12 to 18 months from the time of sowing, a little plant with the first leaves will develop.

The first blooming will take place, according to the species, from 5 to 12 years later, but the long wait is compensated by the beauty and value of the flower and by the long duration of the plant.

Orchids multiply by the fractioning of the rhizome, ensuring to the new plant at least two pseudobulbs; by division of the shoots; and by fragments of the stem provided with roots.

164

165

166

167

168

169

Laelias

Laelia is considered to be a most beautiful and much appreciated genus in the Orchidaceae family; it includes about 40 species and an indefinite number of hybrids that are both interspecific and intergeneric.

Morphology. *Laelia* flowers are large and flashy, single or in terminal racemes, and are generally scented. They have subequal, lanceolate, both free and united sepals; the petals are longer and larger, generally plain, with a more or less distinctive trilobous labellum. The colours are very delicate.

Cultivation. They are grown in the greenhouse with a mild temperature (never below 60°F at night during the winter) with a high humidity.

Watering must be frequent, even more frequent in spring (about every two days), and then less frequent after blooming during their period of rest. Water having the same temperature as the air is always used. Sprinklings of the ground

164-166. Orchid flowers of *Cattleya* and *Laelia cattleya* are without doubt the most elegant ones for shape and colour.

167. A *Cattleya*.

168-169. Imagine what the humid equatorial forests look like by admiring the peculiar beauty of these orchids.

170. *Cattleya* growing in the greenhouse.

favour high humidity as does a pool from which water evaporates continuously.

Strong air draughts are to be avoided, even though an exchange of air is necessary to avoid the condensation of water on the glass. Shading is gradually increased from March to May.

In the beginning of autumn, remove the shade since the light has to be increased for blooming. Repotting is not done at fixed dates, but when the plants really need it. This becomes obvious when new shoots with roots develop and reach the edges of the pot or when there are many shoots on the rhizome and the old ones have to be eliminated. Another task that may be done before vegetation resumption consists of substituting some fresh sphagnum on top without repotting the plants; this has to be done carefully. The most suitable mixture for *Laelias* (also for *Cattleyas* and related types) is made of sphagnum and osmunda fibre in the ratio of 1:2.

Laelia may be grown together with orchids having similar demands. In a temperate greenhouse, species and hybrids of *Laelia*, *Cattleya*, *Brassavola* can be grown together, as well as some *Cymbidium*, *Coelogyne*, *Acineta*, *Houlletia* and in the coldest parts a few *Stanhopea*.

Species and varieties. There are numerous species of *Laelia*. *L. albida*, from Mexico, with scented flowers that are white with a pale pink-coloured labellum that is striped or yellow in the centre.

L. anceps, from Mexico, has pink-lilac flowers which are purple shaded with dark red labellum.

L. crispa, from Brazil, has large flowers that are pure white or shaded with lilac; the crinkled labellum is crimson coloured and velveted.

L. pumila, native to Brazil, has large and solitary, scented flowers that are rose-purple with a purple-crimson labellum and a yellow throat.

L. purpurata, among the largest cultivated orchids has white flowers and a purple labellum.

L. xanthina has yellow flowers with a whitish lip suffused with purple.

Vanda

This is another large and important genus of the Orchidaceae family.

Origin. These are old world plants, native primarily to the Himalayas, Burma, China, India, the Philippines and the South Sea Islands.

Morphology. Epiphytic plants, they are without pseudobulbs and have an erect and leafy stem; the leaves are distichous, rather fleshy or leathery, plain and sometimes cylindrical. The flowers are large, attached to simple and coloured racemes. The sepals are free and spreading and similar to the petals; the labellum is trilobous and inserted in the base of the column; on the lower part, it is elongated, forming a sac or terminating in a spur; the lateral lobes are upright and the median lobe is enlarged and oblong. The flowers are thick and scented. Their capsules are oblong with longitudinal ribbings.

Cultivation. The cultivation of *Vanda* is varied, and is dependent on its particular origin. Almost all the best varieties need a warm greenhouse and demand high humidity, as well as full exposure to light. They are grown in a mixture of sphagnum and osmunda fibre.

Species and varieties. The most important species include the following: *Vanda Sanderiana*, from the Philippines, has white or pinkish flowers that have red spots, with a small yellow labellum leaving red or purple stripes.

V. teres, with white-pinkish coloured petals, yellow lateral lobes with little red dots, and a purple-pink median lobe.

V. caerulea is a species that may be 3 to 4 feet tall; its flowers have pale blue petals that are dark veined and have a dark blue labellum.

171-173. The structure of orchid flowers is almost unchanged in each one of the species that form this large and selected group of Monocotyledons.

Cymbidium

The species of this genus were among the first to be cultivated by man.

Origins. These are epiphytic, semi-epiphytic, or terrestrial plants, originating from tropical Asiatic regions, from Southern China, from India, from Africa and from Australia.

Morphology. They have short robust pseudobulbs and a leafy stem. The long floriferous, erect, curved or pendulous scape bears flowers that are shortly peduncled in lateral racemes. The petals are irregular and the labellum has bright colours and is turned downward.

Species and varieties. *Cymbidium insigne* has rose flowers; *C. Lowianum* has yellow-green coloured flowers; *C. grandiflorum* is a winter blooming type; its flowers are olive-green; *C. Sinense* has fragrant yellowish-brown flowers.

Cultivation. *Cymbidium* are grown in a cool greenhouse. They are relatively easy to grow. Soil is a mixture of top soil, osmunda fibre and decayed oak or beech leaves.

During the summer the plants should be syringed freely and the sun heat of the greenhouse can then be allowed to rise to as much as 80°F. Feed with weak liquid manure in summer.

Cypripedium

The species is commonly called Lady Slipper's Orchid or Moccasin Flower.

Origins. There are about 50 species originating in the East from Hong Kong to India.

Morphology. They are all terrestrial, herbaceous plants, having a stem that is sometimes reduced. The flower is isolated or in an inflorescence carried by a scape that emerges from the centre of the leaves. Characteristic of the flower is the sac-shaped or slipper-shaped labellum. The name *Cypripedium* is erroneously applied to some species, including some so-called *Selenipediums*.

174

175

176

177

178

Species and varieties. The following species are commonly grown:

Cypripedium barbatum, native to Southern India and Java, with white and lilac flowers that are rayed with violet and have a dark violet labellum.

C. faireanum, that comes from North Eastern India and has a very large and solitary flower that is light green coloured and is scattered with violet on the labellum and on the lateral petals; the back petal is large, white-greenish with longitudinal purple stripes.

C. insigne, native to Nepal, has light green flowers and a reddish labellum; the back petal is edged with white and has a green centre and purple spots.

C. delenatii, native to North Vietnam, is uniformly pale pink and scented.

C. Calceolus, native to England, Europe and northern Asia, is dark brown with a yellow lip.

C. japonicum, native to Japan, has solitary greenish-white petals with red dots, and a white and crimson lip.

179

Paphiopedilum

This is a genus of Orchidaceae that is very close to the *Cypripedium* in appearance.

Origins. They are native to Eastern Asia, the Philippines, Malaysia and Malacca. They are mostly terrestrial, even though they are sometimes epiphytic.

Morphology. They are stemless plants with a short rhizome, having only a few, sword-like, leathery, uniformly green or spotted leaves. The flowers are large and brilliant and are on a scape that starts from the centre of the leaves with one or two flowers.

Species and varieties. *Paphiopedilum insigne* is one of the most popular orchids; the flower is green and veined with brown. *P. Rothschildianum*, native to New Guinea, has a magnificent flower; *P. paestans*, from New Guinea, has yellow petals whose edges display purple warts; *P. purpuratum*, has white petals shaded with green and purplish red, dorsal striped. *P. Stonei* is famous for its beautiful varieties and has one of the largest blooms.

Cultivation. *Paphiopedilum* can be cultivated in a temperate greenhouse following the rules that we have indicated at the opening of the chapter. The most suitable substratum is a mixture of sphagnum, osmunda fibre and soil. Varieties are numerous and generally more showy than the species.

180

174, 176, 177. Flowers of *Paphiopedilum*.

175, 178. Two different forms of flowers of the *Cypripedium* genus.

179. Geraniums being grown in a hot bed.

180. Flower bed with *Begonia semperflorens*.

181-182. *Cymbidium* are orchids whose flowers are carried on arching stems.

181

182

184

183

186

185

Greenhouses

As a general rule the bigger the greenhouse, the simpler it is to maintain an even temperature and atmosphere suitable for growing. A very small greenhouse gets hot quickly but it also cools off quickly. Bear this in mind when making a decision about size.

A greenhouse provides many opportunities to grow plants of all kinds and for sowing seeds intended later for the outdoor garden.

Every gardener will develop his own plant interests and collections. There is no end to the opportunities available to the greenhouse owner. He can grow plants that are native to many parts of the world and by regulating the greenhouse environment and his cultural practices, he may have flowers every day in the year, an immensely satisfying reward. And for many people, work in the greenhouse is the ideal method of relaxing.

183. Interior of a greenhouse: on the benches there are plants of *Coleus*, *Begonias*, *Alternanthera*; orchids are in the hanging pots.

184. Greenhouses and hot beds are heated in winter.

185. View in a greenhouse.

186. Close-up of a hot bed.